Vocabulary 8
For Young Catholics

Written by
Seton Staff

Seton Press
Front Royal, VA

Executive Editor: Dr. Mary Kay Clark
Editors: Seton Staff
Illustrator: Benjamin Hatke

© 2018 Seton Home Study School
All rights reserved.
Printed in the United States of America.

Seton Home Study School
1350 Progress Drive
Front Royal, VA 22630
540-636-9990
540-636-1602 fax

For more information, visit us on the Web at http://www.setonhome.org.
Contact us by e-mail at info@setonhome.org.

ISBN: 978-1-60704-119-1

Cover: *Christ Among the Doctors,* Vasily Dmitrievich Polenov

J.M.J.

DEDICATED TO THE SACRED HEART OF JESUS

J.M.J.

Vocabulary 8 for Young Catholics

CONTENTS

Introduction: Notes for Parents vii
Lesson 1: From Bland to Grand 1
Lesson 2: Homer's Antique and Curio Shop 5
Lesson 3: A Self-Fulfilling Prophecy 9
Lesson 4: Haymarket Square 1 13
Lesson 5: Haymarket Square 2 17
Lesson 6: Beware: Tricky Words 21
Lesson 7: Some Assembly Required 25
Lesson 8: Say Again! 1 29
Lesson 9: Say Again! 2 33
Lesson 10: The Miser and the Pauper 1 37
Lesson 11: The Miser and the Pauper 2 41
Lesson 12: It's Greek to Me! 45
Lesson 13: Bon Appetit! 49
Lesson 14: Desert Desolation 1 53
Lesson 15: Desert Desolation 2 57
Lesson 16: Harmony in Diversity 61
Lesson 17: The Runaway 65
Lesson 18: Whatever Floats Your Boat 1 69
Lesson 19: Whatever Floats Your Boat 2 73
Lesson 20: The Storyteller 77

Glossary 81
Answer Key 88

J.M.J.

Notes for Parents

Preface

It is important for students to learn new words as well as different meanings of words they already know. It is also important for students to remember the new vocabulary words and definitions and to apply them in their speaking and writing. In this grade level, students are writing answers to specific questions as well as writing sentences in their other courses, and the vocabulary words studied in this book will enhance those assignments.

With the beginning reading selection in each lesson, our purpose is to motivate students to want to learn new vocabulary words or different meanings of words. The beginning reading selection is meant to be fun and entertaining. The reading usually contains a playful twist and incorporates fifteen vocabulary words. Not only are the reading selections fun to read, but they are purposeful. Students are more apt to learn the meaning of vocabulary words when they see them in the context of sentences, or in the context of an entertaining story.

Besides learning new words, or different meanings for words, students need to practice using words so they remember them over time. Repetition helps memorization. You will notice we have several exercises: looking up the words in a dictionary, identifying words in a list, comparing similar words and contrasting opposite words, using words in sentences, identifying words for a crossword puzzle, and an optional exercise using the thesaurus to find synonyms and antonyms. Seton sells the *Merriam-Webster's Intermediate Thesaurus*.

We believe students will become familiar with these words and comfortable enough with the words to use them in their speech and writing. Seton encourages you, the parent, to think about using these words in daily conversation, especially during the week your student is studying these words.

Notice that sometimes we use a word, such as an adjective, but the main entry in the dictionary will be a noun. In most cases, the adjective is included in the dictionary citation under the noun form of the word. We usually use the form of the word in the list of words in the same part of speech used in the reading selection, but sometimes we use the main form of the word, such as the infinitive form of a verb instead of a past tense. The sentence exercise usually uses the same form as in the main list of words.

Lesson Contents

Reading Selection: This is a simple, usually entertaining story that incorporates practical vocabulary words. The story appeals to students, and the words make sense to them.

Exercise A: This is a list of vocabulary words and their part of speech. Students learn to look up words in the dictionary, to pronounce them correctly, and to locate the definition which is appropriate for the particular use in the reading selection.

Exercise B: This is a list of words usually related to a specified situation. This exercise is intended to help the student see that the meaning of a word often can be determined through a relationship.

Exercise C: These are word groups that further comprehension. The student must think about each word's meaning and match the two words that have either similar meanings or opposite meanings.

An optional thesaurus exercise is also suggested. As the student uses a thesaurus, he further expands his vocabulary as he learns synonyms and antonyms for the lesson's vocabulary word.

Exercise D: These are sentences that require students to remember and to apply the words they have learned in the lesson. Most of these sentences are related to the Catholic Faith or Catholic life, following the directives of the Vatican regarding Catholic schools and textbooks used in Catholic schools.

Crossword Puzzle: This is a popular exercise with students. This exercise is an enjoyable and rewarding way to recall the words they have used.

Answer Key: Located in the back of the book, the key contains answers for Exercises B, C, and D of each lesson.

Suggested Procedure

Notice that there are five lessons per quarter. A quarter review test may be given at any time during the six, seventh, eighth, or ninth week of the quarter. Seton's lesson plans include a quarter review test.

We encourage parents to give a weekly quiz, the parent giving the definition and asking the student to write out the correct vocabulary word. Seton's lesson plans include weekly quizzes.

Each lesson may be completed within one week. It is up to the parent to determine whether the student should cover the exercises in three, four, or five days. Keep in mind that review, repetition, and application over several days helps the definitions to be more easily retained in the memory.

Approach 1: Complete one lesson in a week. First, the student reads the reading selection and then underlines in the reading the vocabulary words from the list in Exercise A. During the week, complete Exercises A through D and the Crossword Puzzle. At the end of the week, the student takes a weekly quiz administered and graded by the parent. There are five lessons for each quarter.

Approach 2: Complete one lesson in a week. First, the student reads the reading selection and then underlines in the reading the vocabulary words from the list in Exercise A. Next, complete the Crossword Puzzle. Students love crossword puzzles. However, students should not copy the definitions for the puzzle in writing the definitions for Exercise A, primarily because students need to practice using the dictionary. During the remainder of the week, complete Exercises A through D. At the end of the week, the student takes a weekly quiz administered and graded by the parent. There are five lessons for each quarter.

Continuous Development: This vocabulary book provides your child a method to learn new vocabulary words. Whenever he encounters an unfamiliar word in his leisure or academic readings, he will know to examine the word within the context of the reading, and to locate it in a dictionary for pronunciation and its appropriate definition. Since this book has five lessons for each nine-week quarter, the student may devote the extra time to his other courses or enjoy leisure reading. Time devoted to leisure reading will continue to expand your child's vocabulary far beyond the words studied in these lessons.

Using the Dictionary and Thesaurus

There are vitally important lessons to be learned in using a dictionary: reviewing alphabetical order past the 1st, 2nd, or 3rd letter; using the Guide Words to locate words; noticing the Guide Words after finding the word; reading and discovering the different meanings one word can have; discovering the different parts of speech for a single word. For the majority of words in this book, words can be found in an intermediate or school dictionary. However, be alert and look for other forms of the word if necessary.

We encourage students to use a thesaurus. A thesaurus contains numerous words with related meanings, each having its own distinct meaning. When your student does any writing, encourage him or her to use a "new" word from the thesaurus. See if you can help your child to understand the small differences in synonyms. An optional thesaurus exercise is suggested in Exercise C. Encourage your student to use or think about different words as you speak together throughout the day. This develops analytical skills to a higher degree.

Finally, we hope you and your student enjoy the playful stories and illustrations in this book.

LESSON 1

FROM BLAND TO GRAND

What makes a bland composition inviting to read? For that matter, what turns a topic that should leave readers thunderstruck into a humdrum composition? Quite simply, words do. A little creativity can help a writer enhance dull writing and make it appealing. For example, *"This movie is totally boring"* might become, *"This movie is better than a sedative; it is an outright cure for insomnia!"* Conversely, *"This is an interesting book"* might read, instead, *"This book is so gripping that eating and sleeping will become secondary!"* Succinct statements can capture a reader's attention just as effectively. For example, *"Two words apply to this movie: "Don't bother!"* For an interesting book, one might write: *"Caution: This book mesmerizes."* Use words well, then, and captivate your readers.

EXERCISE A — In the reading above, underline the words (or form of words) that appear in the list below. Based on the meaning in the reading above, write the dictionary definition for the specific part of speech (noun, verb, adjective, adverb, or preposition) as identified in the list.

1. bland (adj.) _____
2. inviting (adj.) _____
3. thunderstruck (adj.) _____
4. humdrum (adj.) _____
5. creativity (n.) _____
6. enhance (v.) _____
7. outright (adj.) _____
8. insomnia (n.) _____
9. conversely (adv.) _____
10. grip (v.) _____
11. secondary (adj.) _____
12. succinct (adj.) _____
13. capture (v.) _____
14. mesmerize (v.) _____
15. captivate (v) _____

J.M.J.

EXERCISE B Circle the correct word.

1. Which word might describe a short but complete message?
   a) humdrum   b) secondary   c) conversely   d) succinct

2. Which word relates to the opposite side of a point of view?
   a) conversely   b) secondary   c) outright   d) inviting

3. Which word applies to a talent for using one's imagination effectively?
   a) insomnia   b) creativity   c) outright   d) inviting

4. Which word applies to someone who wakes up every night after only three hours of sleep?
   a) humdrum   b) thunderstruck   c) insomnia   d) mesmerize

5. Which word may describe a tedious or boring task?
   a) inviting   b) succinct   c) humdrum   d) creative

EXERCISE C Circle two words which have either similar or opposite meanings. Write the letter **S** if they are similar, or **O** if they are opposite. *Optional:* Use a thesaurus for more synonyms and antonyms for Exercise A words.

1. attractive   inviting   captivate   enhance   _____
2. succinct   grip   thunderstruck grasp   _____
3. mesmerize   outright   somewhat   enhance   _____
4. captivate   improve   bland   enhance   _____
5. thunderstruck   secondary   charm   captivate   _____

Jesus, Mary, Joseph, I love You!   Vocabulary 8 for Young Catholics

EXERCISE D Write on the line the correct list word to complete each sentence.

The splendid assortment of food on the banquet table looks most __ to the hungry guests.	1. _____
In only a few __ statements, the manager gave his workers their orders.	2. _____
"That is an __ lie," the defendant said of the witness' statement.	3. _____
Although Eileen suffers from __ , she can remain alert at work.	4. _____
Peter was __ by Our Lord's words. "No, Lord! I will never deny you!" he responded.	5. _____
Jesus told the Pharisees to give Caesar his due and, __ , to render to God what is God's.	6. _____
The soup was so __ that it had almost no flavor.	7. _____
Dynamic speakers quickly __ an audience and hold their attention.	8. _____
Dad drove carefully in the pouring rain. "Arriving on time is __ to our safety," he said.	9. _____
Magicians are able to __ children with their magic tricks.	10. _____
"I do not need to __ His robe," the woman thought, "I need only touch the hem of His garment.	11. _____
A smile can __ anyone's appearance.	12. _____
Shirley has a keen ability to __ the full meaning of a poem.	13. _____
For Frank, it was just another __ day until his cousin Sally arrived to liven the scene.	14. _____
With a little __ , Mom transformed one corner of the living room into a convincing Nativity scene.	15. _____

CROSSWORD PUZZLE

Use the words from this lesson to complete the crossword puzzle.

ACROSS

1. concise; short and to the point
8. to improve; to increase the quality of something
9. lacking excitement; boring
12. originality
13. to charm; to win someone over
14. to hold firmly; to grasp
15. complete; absolute

DOWN

2. to catch
3. sleeplessness
4. in reversed order
5. stunned; shocked
6. of lesser importance
7. to make spellbound; to transfix
10. plain; unlikely to be noticed
11. appealing; attractive

LESSON 2

HOMER'S ANTIQUE AND CURIO SHOP!

Mr. Sawyer has an uncanny ability to discern junk from treasure. In Homer's shop, he quickly determines that there is a dearth of treasures among the sundry items that others have relinquished there. Among the junk, however, one knife draws his attention. It is dirty and it has a conspicuous blemish, an unsightly paint stain on the handle. He realizes, though, that this knife is invaluable because it is a rare original. Adjacent to it is another knife. This one is gleaming and flawless, but it is a paltry replica. There are other knives that are devoid of blemishes, but most of those are of dubious value as well. Mr. Sawyer buys the first knife and leaves Homer's shop certain that he has a treasure to add to his collection.

EXERCISE A — In the reading above, underline the words (or form of words) that appear in the list below. Based on the meaning in the reading above, write the dictionary definition for the specific part of speech (noun, verb, adjective, adverb, or preposition) as identified in the list.

1. curio (n.) _____
2. uncanny (adj.) _____
3. discern (v.) _____
4. dearth (n.) _____
5. sundry (adj.) _____
6. relinquish (v.) _____
7. conspicuous (adj.) _____
8. blemish (n.) _____
9. unsightly (adj.) _____
10. invaluable (adj.) _____
11. adjacent (adj.) _____
12. paltry (adj.) _____
13. replica (n.) _____
14. devoid (adj.) _____
15. dubious (adj.) _____

J.M.J.

EXERCISE B Circle the correct word.

1. Which word describes a characteristic that stands out?
   a) conspicuous   b) uncanny   c) imagination   d) sundry

2. Which word may apply to items in a "junk drawer"?
   a) invaluable   b) sundry   c) devoid   d) adjacent

3. Which word may apply to an item in a gift shop?
   a) dearth   b) discern   c) relinquish   d) curio

4. Which word applies to the ability to tell whether a statement is false or true?
   a) blemish   b) relinquish   c) discern   d) dubious

5. Which word relates to two buildings that are side by side?
   a) unsightly   b) adjacent   c) uncanny   d) paltry

EXERCISE C Circle two words which have either similar or opposite meanings. Write the letter **S** if they are similar, or **O** if they are opposite. *Optional:* Use a thesaurus for more synonyms and antonyms for Exercise A words.

1. devoid   dubious   paltry   certain   _____
2. dearth   blemish   replica   original   _____
3. unsightly   uncanny   ugly   conspicuous   _____
4. devoid   worthless sundry   invaluable   _____
5. dearth   scarcity   relinquish blemish   _____

Jesus, Mary, Joseph, I love You!

Write on the line the correct list word to complete each sentence.

King Solomon was known for his _ gift of wisdom.	1.
Solomon was able to _ right from wrong.	2.
St. Damien looked beyond the _ sores of lepers.	3.
What mattered to Damien was that their souls be without _.	4.
Our Lord asked the rich young man to _ all his possessions.	5.
The prodigal son felt _ in his worn clothes.	6.
Job's trials resulted in a _ of material things.	7.
Still, Job considered his losses as _ compared to the great love of God.	8.
St. James tells us that faith _ of good works is dead.	9.
Many Catholic homes have a _ of the statue of the Pieta.	10.
Often, a statue of St. Paul stands _ to one of St. Peter.	11.
The gift shop displays _ religious items such as medals, statues, and rosaries.	12.
Our family owns a _, a small horse carved by our great-grandfather.	13.
The old red velvet chair is of _ worth.	14.
For us, however, its sentimental worth is _.	15.

CROSSWORD PUZZLE

Use the words from this lesson to complete the crossword puzzle.

ACROSS

2 lacking
6 next to
9 of great worth; priceless
10 ugly
13 copy; duplicate of an original
14 questionable
15 various; mixed selection

DOWN

1 eerie; mysterious
3 small supply; scarcity
4 imperfection; flaw
5 to distinguish; to tell the difference
7 to give up or give over; to let go
8 attracting attention; obvious
11 of little importance or value; trivial
12 object that is rare or interesting or unusual

LESSON 3

A SELF-FULFILLING PROPHECY

People often describe the behavior of my friend Oliver as erratic. He seems to have a natural inclination to being changeable. Oliver can veer from one direction to another as abruptly as a squirrel. Not only can he suddenly change course, he can, all of a sudden, diverge from a topic during a conversation or significantly alter his plans. This quirk often stupefies those around him.

Generally, people do not comprehend why Oliver can be so susceptible to making sudden changes. One explanation may lie in his name. Oliver's unexpected actions might be unavoidable, and it may not be possible to ever anticipate his next move. The boy may feel compelled to fulfill what his name implies. Oliver's full name, you see, is Oliver Sudden.

EXERCISE A — In the reading above, underline the words (or form of words) that appear in the list below. Based on the meaning in the reading above, write the dictionary definition for the specific part of speech (noun, verb, adjective, adverb, or preposition) as identified in the list.

1. behavior (n.) _____
2. inclination (n.) _____
3. changeable (adj.) _____
4. veer (v.) _____
5. course (n.) _____
6. diverge (v.) _____
7. quirk (n.) _____
8. stupefy (v.) _____
9. susceptible (adj.) _____
10. unexpected (adj.) _____
11. unavoidable (adj.) _____
12. anticipate (v.) _____
13. compel (v.) _____
14. fulfill (v.) _____
15. imply (v.) _____

Circle the correct word.

1. Which word suggests suddenly changing a course of direction?
   a) imply   b) compel   c) veer   d) anticipate

2. Which word relates to realizing a dream or to meet an obligation?
   a) imply   b) fulfill   c) stupefy   d) anticipate

3. Which word applies to the direction one has decided to take?
   a) course   b) inclination   c) behavior   d) quirk

4. Which word relates to a suggestion rather than an outright statement?
   a) diverge   b) unexpected   c) stupefy   d) imply

5. Which word applies to stocking up on food and water when a bad storm is predicted?
   a) unexpected   b) veer   c) anticipate   d) compel

Circle two words which have either similar or opposite meanings. Write the letter S if they are similar, or O if they are opposite. *Optional:* Use a thesaurus for more synonyms and antonyms for Exercise A words.

1. behavior   action   course   quirk   _____
2. fulfill   compel   suggest   stupefy   _____
3. diverge   inclination   changeable   predictable   _____
4. unexpected   unavoidable   changeable   unforeseen   _____
5. quirk   inclination   unavoidable tendency   _____

J.M.J.

EXERCISE D — Write on the line the correct list word to complete each sentence.

Stephen had to __ to the left to avoid the deer in the middle of the road.	1.
It was a natural __ for Our Lady to obey God's will.	2.
Pilgrims today follow the __ Our Lord took to Calvary.	3.
Near the edge of the forest, you will see where the paths __ .	4.
To __ the needs of the injured man, the Good Samaritan gave the innkeeper instructions for his care.	5.
The __ of the traders at the temple angered Jesus.	6.
Because the weather here is so __ , we never know whether or not we will need an umbrella.	7.
The general's plan, to __ the enemy to retreat, was successful.	8.
Many of the events in the Gospels occurred to __ the prophecies of the Old Testament.	9.
After the illness, Peter was __ to colds.	10.
The storm that so frightened the apostles was ___.	11.
His unusual answers __ his teacher.	12.
Welcome mats at front doors __ hospitality.	13.
Enemy troops were so close that an attack was ___.	14.
Tommy never steps on cracks in a sidewalk; it is a __ of his.	15.

CROSSWORD PUZZLE

Use the words from this lesson to complete the crossword puzzle.

ACROSS

1 to foresee and plan for ahead of time
6 odd habit or characteristic
8 to change direction suddenly
10 likely to give in to an action; having no resistance
12 tendency; a leaning toward a particular thought or action
14 unable to be prevented
15 not seen as likely to happen; not foreseen

DOWN

2 direction; route
3 to force or to pressure someone to do something
4 the way one acts or conducts himself
5 to live up to; to bring to reality something that is promised or understood
7 to suggest as fact something that is not actually stated
9 to move away from a common point
11 likely to become different suddenly
13 to bewilder; to perplex

LESSON 4

HAYMARKET SQUARE - 1

Aunt Kim took me to Boston's Haymarket Square one Saturday morning. It was an experience that is indelibly fixed in my memory. This open-air farmer's market draws throngs of shoppers who bustle and jostle as they maneuver through a maze of stalls and vendors. Sounds, aromas, colors, and shapes overwhelm the senses. There is such an assortment of delectable produce on display, ranging from the banal potato to the exotic papaya, that one hardly knows where to begin. My eyes darted from colossal mounds of melons, garlands of garlic, and crates of fruit bursting with ripeness. With a good-natured laugh, Aunt Kim hooked her arm in mine and said, "Come this way. I want you to meet my friend Patrick."

(To be continued)

EXERCISE A In the reading above, underline the words (or form of words) that appear in the list below. Based on the meaning in the reading above, write the dictionary definition for the specific part of speech (noun, verb, adjective, adverb, or preposition) as identified in the list.

1. indelibly (adv.) _____
2. throng (n.) _____
3. bustle (v.) _____
4. jostle (v.) _____
5. maneuver (v.) _____
6. maze (n.) _____
7. overwhelm (v.) _____
8. assortment (n.) _____
9. delectable (adj.) _____
10. produce (n.) _____
11. banal (adj.) _____
12. exotic (adj.) _____
13. papaya (n.) _____
14. colossal (adj.) _____
15. garland (n.) _____

EXERCISE B

Circle the correct word.

1. Which word relates to a small boat that winds its way around larger vessels to safely reach a dock?
   a) jostle b) overwhelm c) bustle d) maneuver

2. Which word relates to something that is not easily deleted?
   a) delectable b) indelibly c) colossal d) garland

3. Which word may relate to people at a mall at Christmas time?
   a) throng b) maze c) banal d) produce

4. Which word may apply to items displayed at a flea market?
   a) colossal b) papaya c) assortment d) bustle

5. Which word relates to a man desperately making his way through a crowd to catch a train?
   a) maze b) jostle c) produce d) overwhelm

EXERCISE C

Circle two words which have either similar or opposite meanings. Write the letter **S** if they are similar, or **O** if they are opposite. *Optional:* Use a thesaurus for more synonyms and antonyms for Exercise A words.

1. colossal — banal — delectable — exotic — _____
2. colossal — overwhelm — garland — miniscule — _____
3. produce — maze — puzzle — overwhelm — _____
4. delectable — bustle — tasty — overwhelm — _____
5. rush — overwhelm — maneuver — bustle — _____

EXERCISE D Write on the line the correct list word to complete each sentence.

Fresh fruit such as pineapple or __ may be found year-round in Hawaii.	1.
It is not unusual here to see people with a __ of flowers around their necks.	2.
Bouquets of __ flowers such as orchids abound.	3.
On our lawn, we saw about a dozen squirrels __ about looking for acorns.	4.
Next to our tiny rowboat, the yacht appeared ___.	5.
At every Easter, a __ of people descend upon Jerusalem.	6.
The city itself is a __ of winding streets and narrow alleys.	7.
The noise and the aromas may __ the first-time visitor.	8.
It is easier to __ one's way around with the help of a guide.	9.
To reach a vendor, it may be necessary to __ through the crowd.	10.
The local __ includes figs, dates, and olives.	11.
The Easter meal consists of an ___ of special traditional dishes.	12.
Spices make certain foods particularly __.	13.
Without such spices, the same foods would be rather __.	14.
The sights, sounds, and aromas are invariably __ impressed upon the memories of visitors.	15.

CROSSWORD PUZZLE

Use the words from this lesson to complete the crossword puzzle.

ACROSS

3 to overpower
7 to move skillfully to attain a goal
9 in a manner that is impossible to remove or erase
11 crowd; large, packed number of people
13 elongated, edible tropical fruit that contains many black seeds
14 to move about in an energetic or noisy manner
15 unusual; out of the ordinary

DOWN

1 variety; collection of different items
2 to push, elbow, or bump against, usually in a crowd
4 complicated network of paths
5 rope of items such as flowers, fruit, or leaves
6 delicious; highly pleasing
8 extremely large; huge
10 fresh fruit and vegetables
12 unoriginal; ordinary

LESSON 5

HAYMARKET SQUARE - 2

Aunt Kim deftly led me through the crowd to a little man with an impish smile.

"Hello, Kim! You've brought a friend, I see," he said in his affable yet understated manner. His brogue added to the man's delightful mien. As he waited on customers, Aunt Kim said, "Patrick is a playful sort, and he has a secret. I'll give you a hint. He always arranges his produce in a premeditated order. See if you can decipher the code."

My curiosity stoked, I surveyed Patrick's array of fruits and vegetables. I saw nothing lavish or unusual about it. There were potatoes, then avocados, turnips, radishes, Indian corn, cabbage, and kale. My puzzled look prompted Aunt Kim to divulge another clue. "It has to do with spelling," she hinted. After some concentration, I exclaimed, "The first letters of each one spell out his name! P-A-T-R-I-C-K!" "Keep going," she urged. I stepped around the table, and saw onions, mangos, apricots, lettuce, leeks, eggplants, and yams. I grinned with comprehension, and then I heard behind me, "Patrick O'Malley at your service!"

EXERCISE A In the reading above, underline the words (or form of words) that appear in the list below. Based on the meaning in the reading above, write the dictionary definition for the specific part of speech (noun, verb, adjective, adverb, or preposition) as identified in the list.

1. deftly (adv.) _____
2. impish (adj.) _____
3. affable (adj.) _____
4. understated (adj.) _____
5. brogue (n.) _____
6. mien (n.) _____
7. premeditate (v.) _____
8. decipher (v.) _____
9. stoke (v.) _____
10. survey (v.) _____
11. array (n.) _____
12. lavish (adj.) _____
13. kale (n.) _____
14. prompt (v.) _____
15. divulge (v.) _____

EXERCISE B Circle the correct word.

1. Which word may describe one who has a habit of teasing?
   a) impish   b) understated   c) affable   d) lavish

2. Which word relates to successfully creating appealing flower arrangements?
   a) mien   b) deftly   c) lavish   d) stoke

3. Which word applies to deliberately planning a course of action?
   a) decipher   b) stoke   c) premeditate   d) prompt

4. Which word may describe people we enjoy having around us?
   a) lavish   b) mien   c) array   d) affable

5. Which word relates to a display of goods in a store window?
   a) mien   b) array   c) kale   d) brogue

EXERCISE C Circle two words which have either similar or opposite meanings. Write the letter **S** if they are similar, or **O** if they are opposite. *Optional:* Use a thesaurus for more synonyms and antonyms for Exercise A words.

1. premeditate   hide   divulge   prompt   _____
2. stoke   study   survey   mien   _____
3. deftly   premeditate   prompt   urge   _____
4. affable   understated   array   lavish   _____
5. stoke   decipher   extinguish   impish   _____

J.M.J.

Write on the line the correct list word to complete each sentence.

A priest will not ___ what is said in the confessional.	1.
Because he is so ___, our pastor makes people feel at ease.	2.
Born of Irish parents, he speaks with a slight ___.	3.
Courtesy and kindness ___ his every action.	4.
The archeologist tried to ___ the writing on the cave wall.	5.
The scout used a dry twig to ___ the small campfire.	6.
We called a team of experts to ___ the damage from the storm.	7.
The father gave a ___ banquet for his prodigal son who repented.	8.
The jeweler ___ repaired the delicate mechanism in the antique watch.	9.
Our kitten makes us laugh with her ___ antics.	10.
Aunt Mildred served ham with a side dish of ___.	11.
The candidate's arrogant ___ turned people against him.	12.
Our booth at the fair displayed an appealing ___ of baked goods.	13.
The hall was tastefully decorated with an ___ elegance.	14.
They failed to ___ a route of evacuation during a fire.	15.

19 Vocabulary 8 for Young Catholics   Jesus, Mary, Joseph, I love You!

CROSSWORD PUZZLE

Use the words from this lesson to complete the crossword puzzle.

ACROSS

1. expressed or done in a simple way
5. manner; conduct; behavior
6. extravagant; elaborate
8. to decode; to figure out the meaning
10. friendly; good-natured; easy-going around people
13. certain order or arrangement of items
14. to stir up; to kindle
15. to look at carefully and in an investigative way

DOWN

2. to reveal; to make known
3. to think about and plan carefully ahead of time
4. mischievous; tricky in a playful way
7. in a skillful manner
9. to cause to do something
11. manner of speaking characteristic of the Irish
12. variety of cabbage

LESSON 6

BEWARE: TRICKY WORDS

The guests compliment the hostess on the flowers in the centerpiece that complement the color of the table linens.

Do not back down from a principle. Remember that charity is the principal virtue.

A sad story is often touching. A person who is often sad may be touchy.

The gray horse with the white bridle will pull the carriage for the bridal party.

Wyatt Earp is noted as an upright lawman who fought notorious outlaws.

The high incidence of successive storms last winter resulted in an increased number of incidents of power outages. Repairmen were successful in restoring power everywhere.

A fable is a story that alludes to a lesson to be learned. Sometimes the lesson may elude the reader and it must be explained to him.

EXERCISE A In the reading above, underline the words (or form of words) that appear in the list below. Based on the meaning in the reading above, write the dictionary definition for the specific part of speech (noun, verb, adjective, adverb, or preposition) as identified in the list.

1. compliment (v.) _____
2. complement (v.) _____
3. principle (n.) _____
4. principal (adj.) _____
5. touching (adj.) _____
6. touchy (adj.) _____
7. bridle (n.) _____
8. bridal (adj.) _____
9. noted (adj.) _____
10. notorious (adj.) _____
11. incidence (n.) _____
12. successive (adj.) _____
13. incident (n.) _____
14. allude (v.) _____
15. elude (v.) _____

EXERCISE B Circle the correct word.

1. Which word may apply to a story that makes us tearful?
   a) bridal   b) touchy   c) noted   d) touching

2. Which word may relate to several events occurring in a row?
   a) notable   b) incident   c) successive   d) principal

3. Which word may describe the gangster Al Capone?
   a) notorious   b) noted   c) principal   d) touching

4. Which word applies to what motivates our words and actions?
   a) complement   b) principle   c) incidence   d) bridle

5. Which word applies to what helps us feel good about ourselves?
   a) allude   b) incident   c) compliment   d) touching

EXERCISE C Circle two words which have either similar or opposite meanings. Write the letter **S** if they are similar, or **O** if they are opposite. **Optional:** Use a thesaurus for more synonyms and antonyms for Exercise A words.

1. bridal   bridle   harness   complement   _____
2. principal   unknown   noted   allude   _____
3. touching   elude   principal   insignificant _____
4. elude   allude   complement   suggest   _____
5. happening   elude   complement   incident   _____

EXERCISE D — Write on the line the correct list word to complete each sentence.

A flower girl tosses petals along the ___ path.	1.
Guests ___ the bride.	2.
A pearl necklace will usually ___ a bride's dress perfectly.	3.
Pharaoh became ___ for his abuse of the Israelites.	4.
Each plague upon the Egyptians was a horrible ___.	5.
The parting of the Red Sea enabled the Israelites to ___ Pharaoh's soldiers.	6.
Jesus taught the ___ of loving others as we love ourselves.	7.
There is a high ___ of crime in that rundown neighborhood.	8.
We say ten ___ Hail Marys in each decade of the Rosary.	9.
In the Bible, Job is ___ for his trust in God amid his afflictions.	10.
The high priest was the ___ leader of the Jewish communities.	11.
The love of the father for his prodigal son is quite ___.	12.
Because she was so ___, Karen did not take criticism well.	13.
Many New Testament passages ___ to Old Testament prophecies.	14.
The centurion led his horse by its ___.	15.

CROSSWORD PUZZLE

Use the words from this lesson to complete the crossword puzzle.

ACROSS

6 basic truth; rule or belief that governs one's behavior
7 main; of greatest importance
9 to escape one's grasp or understanding
10 overly sensitive; easily hurt
11 part of the harness that fits over the head of a horse
12 event; occurrence
14 causing feelings of sympathy or tenderness
15 rate or frequency of occurrence

DOWN

1 related to a bride or a wedding
2 to refer to without actually naming
3 one after another
4 to express praise or admiration or approval
5 to complete or to make perfect
8 well-known in an unfavorable way
13 well-known and respected

LESSON 7

SOME ASSEMBLY REQUIRED

George was excited as the delivery man set down a large box at his door.

"Great! It's my new CD/DVD shelving unit! I'm going to put it together right now."

The project did not seem to require an inordinate amount of skill. Since George was rather adroit anyway, he examined the components and ascertained that the task would be rather straightforward. George also could be persevering and indefatigably resolute, so he was certain he could successfully assemble the shelving unit.

Three hours later, however, George's exuberance had dissipated and turned into consternation, and, clearly, George was rankled. He had dismantled sections of the unit four times already because he had omitted certain requisite steps. He unfolded the directions, and begrudgingly conceded, "When all else fails, follow instructions." Sometime later, as he admired the result of his efforts, he resolved that, next time, he would begin with the directions.

EXERCISE A In the reading above, underline the words (or form of words) that appear in the list below. Based on the meaning in the reading above, write the dictionary definition for the specific part of speech (noun, verb, adjective, adverb, or preposition) as identified in the list.

1. adroit (adj.) _____

2. component (n.) _____

3. ascertain (v.) _____

4. straightforward (adj.) _____

5. indefatigably (adv.) _____

6. resolute (adj.) _____

7. assemble (v.) _____

8. exuberance (n.) _____

9. dissipate (v.) _____

10. consternation (n.) _____

11. rankle (v.) _____

12. dismantle (v.) _____

13. omit (v.) _____

14. requisite (adj.) _____

15. begrudgingly (adv.) _____

EXERCISE B

Circle the correct word.

1. Which word may describe a master carpenter?

   a) straightforward   b) requisite   c) adroit   d) resolute

2. Which word may apply to the way ants gather food for the colony?

   a) begrudgingly   b) indefatigably   c) component   d) requisite

3. Which word may apply to fog lifting as the sun warms the ground?

   a) dissipate   b) dismantle   c) rankle   d) assemble

4. Which word may describe an explanation that everyone can understand?

   a) resolute   b) requisite   c) ascertain   d) straightforward

5. Which word may relate to what a pesky mosquito might do to us?

   a) dismantle   b) rankle   c) assemble   d) ascertain

EXERCISE C

Circle two words which have either similar or opposite meanings. Write the letter **S** if they are similar, or **O** if they are opposite. **Optional:** Use a thesaurus for more synonyms and antonyms for Exercise A words.

1. component   consternation   ascertain   exuberance   _____
2. assemble   rankle   dismantle   ascertain   _____
3. resolute   requisite   include   omit   _____
4. begrudgingly reluctantly   rankle   resolute   _____
5. ascertain   component   requisite   optional   _____

EXERCISE D

Write on the line the correct list word to complete each sentence.

George Washington was ___ in his fight against the British troops.	1.
Matthew and Luke include the Birth of Jesus, but Mark and John ___ it.	2.
Many wanted to ___ that Jesus truly was the Messiah.	3.
In his ___, the blind man danced with joy after Jesus cured him.	4.
Our Lord's popularity served to ___ the Pharisees.	5.
We cannot allow our faith to ___ even amid hardship.	6.
Our Lord's command is ___: "Love one another as I have loved you."	7.
The Pharisees ___ admitted that Jesus spoke the truth.	8.
After the Resurrection, the disciples ___ spread the Good News.	9.
The absence of mortal sin is a ___ condition for receiving Holy Communion.	10.
Roger made sure he had every ___ necessary to build his model airplane.	11.
The tree house was no longer safe, so the boys had to ___ it.	12.
Only an ___ craftsman can produce works of art.	13.
Today, we started to ___ a 5000-piece jigsaw puzzle.	14.
To their ___, the police could find no trace of the burglar.	15.

CROSSWORD PUZZLE

Use the words from this lesson to complete the crossword puzzle.

ACROSS

1. in a resentfully reluctant manner
3. to fit parts together to form a whole
5. to disappear gradually to vanishing; to dissolve
6. untiringly; tirelessly
8. uncomplicated; clear
11. necessary for achieving a particular goal or purpose
12. dismay; feeling of helplessness
14. part of a larger whole

DOWN

2. to take apart
3. skillful with one's hands
4. excitement; lively energy
7. to make sure; to find out for certain
9. to annoy; to irritate
10. determined; unwavering
13. to leave out

LESSON 8

SAY AGAIN? 1

Even proficient speakers and writers unwittingly make blunders. Some errors are subtle, while others are blatant. This lack of accuracy may lead English teachers and editors to rue their choice of professions. Some erroneous or misleading expressions that have become part of our vernacular fall in the category of the oxymoron. These are words that, when used together, seem to oppose each other. Some examples are "rush hour" (when traffic is almost at a standstill), "rapid transit system" (which some people will argue is anything but fast), "jumbo shrimp," and "pretty ugly" (which make some ask, "Well, which one is it?")

The next group is the misnomer. These are words that we misuse to replace exact terms, and many have become commonplace. For example, a blackboard may be green or gray, or even white. We call an adhesive bandage a band-aid, which is a brand name (BAND-AID®). We use yet another brand name, Xerox®, when we make a photocopy of something. Petroleum jelly becomes Vaseline®, and we often call sealable plastic bags Ziploc® bags. (To be continued)

EXERCISE A In the reading above, underline the words (or form of words) that appear in the list below. Based on the meaning in the reading above, write the dictionary definition for the specific part of speech (noun, verb, adjective, adverb, or preposition) as identified in the list.

1. blunder (n.) _____
2. subtle (adj.) _____
3. blatant (adj.) _____
4. accuracy (n.) _____
5. rue (v.) _____
6. erroneous (adj.) _____
7. vernacular (n.) _____
8. oxymoron (n.) _____
9. standstill (n.) _____
10. transit (n.) _____
11. misnomer (n.) _____
12. misuse (v.) _____
13. commonplace (adj.) _____
14. adhesive (adj.) _____
15. photocopy (n.) _____

EXERCISE B Circle the correct word.

1. Which word applies when someone is sorry about a decision he made?
   a) rue   b) subtle   c) standstill   d) commonplace

2. Which word may describe a style of writing that contains many local expressions?
   a) subtle   b) blatant   c) vernacular   d) misnomer

3. Which word relates to a mistaken judgment made about someone?
   a) oxymoron   b) adhesive   c) erroneous   d) accuracy

4. Which word applies when the movement of troops is stalled?
   a) adhesive   b) transit   c) subtle   d) standstill

5. Which word may apply when someone stirs salt instead of sugar in his coffee?
   a) blunder   b) vernacular   c) misnomer   d) transit

EXERCISE C Circle two words which have either similar or opposite meanings. Write the letter **S** if they are similar, or **O** if they are opposite. *Optional:* Use a thesaurus for more synonyms and antonyms for Exercise A words.

1. erroneous   subtle   blatant   commonplace   _____
2. adhesive   photocopy   oxymoron   contradiction   _____
3. accuracy   unusual   adhesive   commonplace   _____
4. rue   transit   misnomer   standstill   _____
5. misnomer   duplicate   photocopy   adhesive   _____

J.M.J.

EXERCISE D Write on the line the correct list word to complete each sentence.

Wise rulers do not ___ their power.	1.
My aunt replicated grandmother's recipe with astonishing ___.	2.
My sister always wakes up in a bad mood; she claims "Good Morning" is an ___.	3.
Heretics preach ___ teachings about the faith.	4.
Huge flags and posters were a ___ expression of their patriotism.	5.
Because of the parade, traffic was at a ___.	6.
Missionaries used the ___ of Native Americans to teach them about God.	7.
Dad paid the bill and then he made a ___ of the receipt.	8.
The difference between the original and the copy were so ___ that we could not tell one from the other.	9.
The chairman mispronounced the main speaker's name; it was an embarrassing ___.	10.
Fortunately, our new computer was not damaged in ___ from the factory.	11.
When we ask for Scotch® tape, we are using a ___ for cellophane tape.	12.
The use of cell phones has become ___.	13.
Early in the story, the heroine thought she would ___ the day she left home.	14.
It will take a strong ___ material to hold together this broken vase.	15.

31 Vocabulary 8 for Young Catholics   Jesus, Mary, Joseph, I love You!

CROSSWORD PUZZLE

Use the words from this lesson to complete the crossword puzzle.

ACROSS

1 to use the wrong way or for the wrong purpose
3 able to stick
6 photographic duplicate of written or printed material produced by the action of light on a specially prepared surface
7 usual; ordinary
11 regret
12 condition in which there is no movement or activity
13 incorrect

DOWN

1 incorrect or inaccurate name or designation
2 difficult to distinguish
4 ordinary language; common or usual speech
5 very obvious
8 correctness; precision
9 carrying of persons or goods from one place to another
10 careless mistake; mistake due to lack of thought, insight, or knowledge

LESSON 9

SAY AGAIN? 2

Another pitfall for writers and speakers is redundancy. This use of superfluous words is more prevalent than one might think because we often interject extra words into our speech without even realizing it.

Consider, for example, "We will meet at 10 a.m. tomorrow morning." Since "a.m." can never mean afternoon or evening, "a.m." and "in the morning" are repetitive. Use one or the other. Another example is, "Let's circle around the neighborhood." There is no other way to circle something than around it. So, delete the word "around." Here are some common redundant expressions: small in size, tall in stature, few in number, at this moment in time. Try to point out the unnecessary words in the following phrases: autobiography of one's life, collaborate together, nape of his neck, passing fad, overused cliché, and vacillate back and forth.

Avoid redundancies. A few well chosen words can go a long way.

EXERCISE A In the reading above, underline the words (or form of words) that appear in the list below. Based on the meaning in the reading above, write the dictionary definition for the specific part of speech (noun, verb, adjective, adverb, or preposition) as identified in the list.

1. pitfall (n.) _____

2. redundancy (n.) _____

3. superfluous (adj.) _____

4. prevalent (adj.) _____

5. interject (v.) _____

6. consider (v.) _____

7. repetitive (adj.) _____

8. delete (v.) _____

9. stature (n.) _____

10. autobiography (n.) _____

11. collaborate (v.) _____

12. nape (n.) _____

13. fad (n.) _____

14. cliché (n.) _____

15. vacillate (v.) _____

EXERCISE B — Circle the correct word.

1. Which word describes some words that we should delete from our compositions?
   a) stature   b) prevalent   c) autobiography   d) superfluous

2. Which word applies when people cooperate on a task?
   a) interject   b) consider   c) vacillate   d) collaborate

3. Which word may apply to a source of temptation?
   a) redundancy   b) pitfall   c) stature   d) cliché

4. Which word may apply when someone keeps changing his mind?
   a) vacillate   b) consider   c) interject   d) repetitive

5. Which word may describe an opinion shared by a majority of people?
   a) repetitive   b) stature   c) prevalent   d) superfluous

EXERCISE C — Circle two words which have either similar or opposite meanings. Write the letter **S** if they are similar, or **O** if they are opposite. **Optional:** Use a thesaurus for more synonyms and antonyms for Exercise A words.

1. consider   nape   interject   omit   _____
2. redundancy   delete   fad   erase   _____
3. consider   dismiss   repetition   fad   _____
4. fad   redundancy   pitfall   repetition   _____
5. pitfall   fad   craze   superfluous   _____

EXERCISE D — Write on the line the correct list word to complete each sentence.

If we __ extra words, our compositions will be crisper and more clear.	1.
Many famous people find help to write their __.	2.
The parishes in our county usually __ on the holiday food drive.	3.
A stole is a vestment that rests on the __.	4.
Our pastor likes to __ humor in his sermons.	5.
The term "pair of twins" is an example of a ___.	6.
The term "a chance of a lifetime" is an example of a __.	7.
A ___ may be popular, but it is usually short-lived.	8.
Father asked the boy to __ a vocation to the priesthood.	9.
We must never __ between right and wrong.	10.
The gospels tell us that Jesus grew in wisdom and in __.	11.
The mayor's speech was not effective because it was long-winded and __.	12.
The washing of a guest's dusty feet was a custom that was __ in the time of Jesus.	13.
If one wears suspenders, a belt is __.	14.
Tantalizing desserts may be a __ for those who want to avoid sugar.	15.

35 Vocabulary 8 for Young Catholics

CROSSWORD PUZZLE

Use the words from this lesson to complete the crossword puzzle.

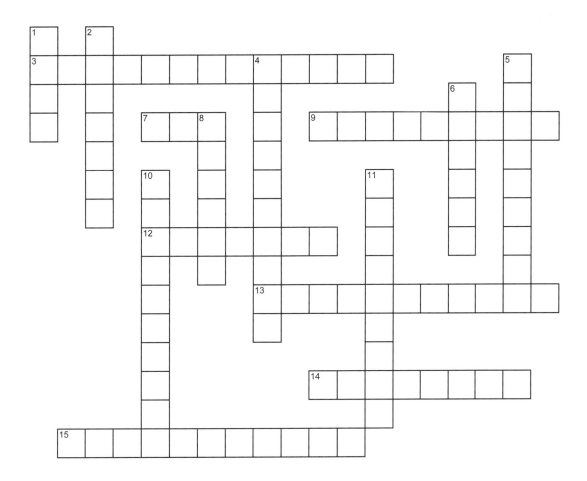

ACROSS

3 a person's written account of his own life
7 short-lived widely held enthusiasm over some practice or interest
9 to waver between one choice and another
12 trap; snare
13 to work jointly on a project or activity
14 to think carefully about
15 extra; unnecessary

DOWN

1 the back of the neck
2 a person's height
4 the use of unnecessary words
5 to place or include among other things
6 word or phrase that becomes stale from overuse
8 to eliminate; to remove
10 marked by being stated or said again
11 widespread

LESSON 10

THE MISER AND THE PAUPER (1)

In his own London slum, Davy was just another nondescript ragamuffin. "You're a good boy," his mother maintained. "Always be honorable. Even a pauper's word and good name are worth more than riches." Davy looked at their humble but clean flat and felt grateful.

Later, the seven-year-old hunkered down between two newsstands at a busy intersection. "Alms, please," he entreated. A pretentious man stopped near Davy and reached into his pocket. Davy timorously held out his hand. The stranger's degrading sneer made Davy cringe.

The man pulled out a card, referred to the address on it, and started toward a nearby building. A bank note had slipped out of the man's pocket with the card. "One pound!" Davy exclaimed to himself, "that's enough to buy bread, a ham bone, a few vegetables for stew—a veritable feast for my mum and me!"

Then Davy recalled his mother's words, "Always be honorable." The man had not given Davy the money. It was not his to keep. But then, the man did not need it nor would he miss it. Davy and his mother were hungry. What should he do?   (To be continued)

EXERCISE A In the reading above, underline the words (or form of words) that appear in the list below. Based on the meaning in the reading above, write the dictionary definition for the specific part of speech (noun, verb, adjective, adverb, or preposition) as identified in the list.

1. nondescript (adj.) _____
2. ragamuffin (n.) _____
3. maintain (v.) _____
4. pauper (n.) _____
5. humble (adj.) _____
6. flat (n.) _____
7. hunker (v.) _____
8. alms (n.) _____
9. entreat (v.) _____
10. pretentious (adj.) _____
11. timorously (adv.) _____
12. degrading (adj.) _____
13. sneer (n.) _____
14. cringe (v.) _____
15. veritable (adj.) _____

EXERCISE B — Circle the correct word.

1. Which word applies when someone holds his own in an argument?
   a) maintain   b) hunker   c) cringe   d) entreat

2. Which word may describe a plain building that blends in with others around it?
   a) pretentious   b) nondescript   c) degrading   d) veritable

3. Which word may relate to desperately requesting something?
   a) hunker   b) cringe   c) humble   d) entreat

4. Which word may relate to the ways of a self-conscious person?
   a) ragamuffin   b) pauper   c) timorously   d) degrading

5. Which word may apply to the expression on an unkind person's face?
   a) cringe   b) sneer   c) entreat   d) veritable

EXERCISE C — Circle two words which have either similar or opposite meanings. Write the letter **S** if they are similar, or **O** if they are opposite. *Optional:* Use a thesaurus for more synonyms and antonyms for Exercise A words.

1. pauper   humble   alms   pretentious   _____
2. hunker   flat   degrading   embarrassing   _____
3. veritable   nondescript   true   degrading   _____
4. sneer   hunker   crouch   entreat   _____
5. ragamuffin   pauper   flat   cringe   _____

Jesus, Mary, Joseph, I love You!

EXERCISE D Write on the line the correct list word to complete each sentence.

People went to Jesus to ___ Him for cures for themselves or loved ones.	1.
Friars used to travel the countryside to collect ___ for the poor.	2.
A ___ played with a top, his only toy.	3.
Because he made unwise financial decisions, the rich man became a ___.	4.
The self-conscious woman ___ approached Jesus.	5.
In order not to get caught, a spy must be ___ in a crowd.	6.
In London, the artist has a ___ on the second floor.	7.
The hunter decided to ___ down in the field and wait for the deer to pass.	8.
Many successful people have come from ___ beginnings.	9.
Three times did Peter ___ he did not know Jesus.	10.
Deafening claps of thunder made the youngster ___.	11.
Guests made ___ remarks about the woman who washed the feet of Jesus.	12.
Gorgeous flower beds and fruit trees made our vacation spot a ___ paradise.	13.
The new manager's ___ airs did not impress anyone.	14.
The villain in a cartoon is easily recognized by the ___ on his face.	15.

39 Vocabulary 8 for Young Catholics

CROSSWORD PUZZLE

Use the words from this lesson to complete the crossword puzzle.

ACROSS

4 to shrink in fear
5 modest; simple
6 very poor person
8 poorly clothed child
9 British term for apartment
12 having no distinctive characteristics
13 scornful smile that shows contempt
14 money for the poor
15 to strongly state to be true or factual; to insist

DOWN

1 in a shy and fearful manner
2 humiliating; causing lack of self-respect
3 true; actual
7 trying to appear more important than one actually is
10 to crouch; to settle in for awhile
11 to ask for earnestly; to beg or plead

LESSON 11

THE MISER AND THE PAUPER (2)

Davy grappled with his dilemma for some seconds. Then he went after the stranger. "This is yours, sir." The man was indignant that this insolent pauper should deign to address him. "It fell out of your pocket when you pulled out that card," Davy explained.

The man's eyes widened in astonishment then narrowed in bewilderment. He could not fathom such a clearly degenerate rogue being completely devoid of guile. He hesitated. His ambivalence evaporated, however, for he was not capable of feeling compassion for the scruffy boy. The miser scornfully snatched the note and shoved it in his pocket. Davy turned away.

He heard someone behind him. "You did well, lad," the man told Davy simply. "Let me shake your hand." Davy timidly shook the stranger's hand, and when he retrieved it, he saw that the stranger had slipped a five pound note in Davy's palm. Confounded, Davy looked up to the stranger, but he was gone. Davy went home feeling somehow older and wiser.

EXERCISE A In the reading above, underline the words (or form of words) that appear in the list below. Based on the meaning in the reading above, write the dictionary definition for the specific part of speech (noun, verb, adjective, adverb, or preposition) as identified in the list.

1. grapple (v.) _____
2. dilemma (n.) _____
3. indignant (adj.) _____
4. insolent (adj.) _____
5. address (v.) _____
6. fathom (v.) _____
7. degenerate (adj.) _____
8. rogue (n.) _____
9. guile (n.) _____
10. ambivalence (n.) _____
11. scruffy (adj.) _____
12. scornfully (adv.) _____
13. timidly (adv.) _____
14. retrieve (v.) _____
15. confounded (adj.) _____

EXERCISE B Circle the correct word.

1. Which word applies when deciding whether to tell someone the truth or spare their feelings?
   a) rogue   b) dilemma   c) guile   d) insolent

2. Which word describes a child who shows no respect for adults?
   a) indignant   b) scruffy   c) confounded   d) insolent

3. Which word applies to trying to understand the culture of a foreign country?
   a) retrieve   b) ambivalence   c) fathom   d) address

4. Which word may apply to a petty thief?
   a) rogue   b) grapple   c) scornfully   d) confounded

5. Which word may apply to someone who is without virtues?
   a) indignant   b) degenerate   c) scruffy   d) confounded

EXERCISE C Circle two words which have either similar or opposite meanings. Write the letter **S** if they are similar, or **O** if they are opposite. *Optional:* Use a thesaurus for more synonyms and antonyms for Exercise A words.

1. indignant   insolent   timorously   timidly   _____
2. guile   scornfully   lovingly   scruffy   _____
3. retrieve   address   regain   grapple   _____
4. honesty   dilemma   ambivalence   guile   _____
5. ambivalence confounded   confused   indignant   _____

EXERCISE D — Write on the line the correct list word to complete each sentence.

Mark could not __ the concept behind the math problem.	1.
After straying for about a week, our dog came back looking quite __.	2.
The prodigal son had become __ after living a life of loose morals.	3.
The Pharisees were __ that Jesus should dare contradict them.	4.
The disciples had to __ with the heavy nets filled with fish.	5.
His followers started to __ Jesus as "Rabbi" ("Teacher").	6.
Jesus felt sorrow over the __ felt by the rich young man.	7.
__, Thomas placed his fingers in Our Lord's side.	8.
When Joseph and Mary found their Son teaching in the temple, they were __.	9.
At Our Lord's crucifixion, one __ thief did not repent.	10.
Instead, that thief spoke __ to Jesus.	11.
Filled with __, Satan is ever ready to deceive us.	12.
Phil dropped the football, but, fortunately, his teammate was able to __ it.	13.
Pilate's __ was whether or not to condemn a Man with Whom he found no fault.	14.
In some novels, a __ mends his ways as the result of the kindness of another.	15.

CROSSWORD PUZZLE

Use the words from this lesson to complete the crossword puzzle.

ACROSS

1. to wrestle; to grasp and struggle with
5. with contempt or disdain
6. showing rudeness and lack of respect
8. to comprehend something strange or puzzling
9. mixed or contradictory feelings
11. to take back; to regain possession of
12. untidy and shabby
13. having lost any desirable qualities

DOWN

1. trickery; dishonesty; deceit
2. confused; perplexed
3. situation that requires a difficult choice between two or more things
4. feeling anger at what seems undeserved treatment
7. with shyness
10. to speak to directly
11. dishonest or tricky person; person without principles

LESSON 12

IT'S GREEK TO ME!

Many English words originate from the Greek language. A Greek prefix or suffix may suggest the meaning of a given English word. The prefix *auto*, for example, means "self." So, "automobile" means a vehicle that "moves itself." The prefixes *hyper* and *pan* mean "excessive" and "all" respectively. Hence, we have the words hyperventilate and panacea.

We form some words by combining two Greek prefixes. The prefix *a* means "without"; used with the prefixes *morph* ("shape") and *path* ("feeling"), we have amorphous and apathy.

Greek suffixes give meanings to words, too. *Graph* means "written down," from which we get such words as cryptograph and seismograph. *Meter* means "measure." The words perimeter and altimeter are derived from this suffix.

Finally, English words sometimes use both a Greek prefix and suffix. The Greek prefixes *bio* ("life") and *geo* ("earth") used with the suffix *logy* give us the words biology and geology.

Knowledge of Greek prefixes and suffixes, then, is very helpful. Refer to those you already know and guess the meanings of graphology, autograph, and pandemic. Amazing, isn't it?

EXERCISE A In the reading above, underline the words (or form of words) that appear in the list below. Based on the meaning in the reading above, write the dictionary definition for the specific part of speech (noun, verb, adjective, adverb, or preposition) as identified in the list.

1. originate (v.) _____

2. respectively (adv.) _____

3. hyperventilate (v.) _____

4. panacea (n.) _____

5. amorphous (adj.) _____

6. apathy (n.) _____

7. cryptograph (n.) _____

8. seismograph (n.) _____

9. perimeter (n.) _____

10. altimeter (n.) _____

11. biology (n.) _____

12. geology (n.) _____

13. graphology (n.) _____

14. autograph (n.) _____

15. pandemic (n.) _____

EXERCISE B Circle the correct word.

1. Which word relates to plants and animals?
   a) seismograph   b) geology   c) graphology   d) biology

2. Which word is something that may be useful in areas prone to earthquakes?
   a) amorphous   b) apathy   c) pandemic   d) seismograph

3. Which word may be something of interest to an FBI agent?
   a) altimeter   b) perimeter   c) cryptograph   d) geology

4. Which word may relate to the result of being frightened out of one's wits?
   a) hyperventilate   b) respectively   c) pandemic   d) amorphous

5. Which word relates to the global outbreak of a flu?
   a) apathy   b) pandemic   c) panacea   d) perimeter

EXERCISE C Circle two words which have either similar or opposite meanings. Write the letter **S** if they are similar, or **O** if they are opposite. *Optional:* Use a thesaurus for more synonyms and antonyms for Exercise A words.

1. pandemic   amorphous   perimeter   shapeless   _____
2. biology   panacea   respectively   randomly   _____
3. graphology   passion   apathy   biology   _____
4. perimeter   altimeter   outline   panacea   _____
5. panacea   originate   geology   cure-all   _____

Jesus, Mary, Joseph, I love You!   Vocabulary 8 for Young Catholics   46

EXERCISE D

Write on the line the correct list word to complete each sentence.

While it is not a ___, aspirin has numerous useful health benefits.	1.
Helena and Augusta are the capitals of Montana and Maine __.	2.
Our new neighbors put up a fence on the __ of their property.	3.
An __ is an essential instrument in an airplane.	4.
I am eager to study the human body in next year's __ course.	5.
Out of __, some people do not read newspapers nor do they bother to vote.	6.
The author's __ is on the title page of that book.	7.
The Spanish influenza was a deadly __.	8.
When Sally pursued __ as a hobby, we gave her samples of our handwriting to analyze.	9.
After three days of unseasonably warm weather, our snowman became an __ blob.	10.
Overcome by anxiety, the patient began to __.	11.
Figs and dates __ from areas with a warm climate.	12.
A __ can alert scientists of an impending earthquake.	13.
An expert who could decode a __ played an essential role in WW II.	14.
__ reveals fascinating facts about how mountain ranges were formed.	15.

CROSSWORD PUZZLE

Use the words from this lesson to complete the crossword puzzle.

ACROSS

1 a person's name handwritten by himself
3 something written in code
4 study of the earth's structure
13 to breathe at an unnaturally fast rate
14 lack of feeling or concern
15 study of living things

DOWN

2 instrument used to measure height or altitude
5 study of handwriting
6 in the order given
7 having no clearly defined shape
8 the length of a line that forms a boundary
9 to come from; to arise from a source
10 cure for any disease; solution for all problems
11 disease that spreads throughout a wide area
12 instrument used to measure vibrations of the earth

LESSON 13

BON APPETIT!

The French know a thing or two about having a good appetite (*bon appétit*). After all, they have been masters of gastronomy for centuries, and they have made an art of gustatory indulgence. If imitation is indeed the most sincere form of flattery, we have flattered the French to the point of adulation by incorporating their very words into our culinary vocabulary.

Let's consider the restaurant, for example. The cook is a chef, and the restaurant owner is a restaurateur. When we order dinner *à la carte*, we select individual items from the menu, the French word for which is *carte*. We may begin with an appetizer, and then choose an entrée and a suitable potable item. Likely entrée choices may be sautéed meat or vegetables or a soufflé. For dessert, a light mousse would be perfect.

There is no need to fear feeling gauche in a restaurant. All it takes is knowledge of some key French words and a *bon appétit*!

EXERCISE A In the reading above, underline the words (or form of words) that appear in the list below. Based on the meaning in the reading above, write the dictionary definition for the specific part of speech (noun, verb, adjective, adverb, or preposition) as identified in the list.

1. gastronomy (n.) _____
2. gustatory (adj.) _____
3. indulgence (n.) _____
4. adulation (n.) _____
5. culinary (adj.) _____
6. chef (n.) _____
7. restaurateur (n.) _____
8. à la carte (adv.) _____
9. appetizer (n.) _____
10. entrée (n.) _____
11. potable (adj.) _____
12. sautéed (adj.) _____
13. soufflé (n.) _____
14. mousse (n.) _____
15. gauche (adj.) _____

Circle the correct word.

1. Which word relates to the area of expertise of a restaurant critic?

    a) indulgence   b) adulation   c) potable   d) gastronomy

2. Which word may describe an awkward person?

    a) gustatory   b) gauche   c) culinary   d) potable

3. Which word relates to partaking in something for enjoyment?

    a) indulgence   b) gustatory   c) appetizer   d) mousse

4. Which word relates to something that may be enjoyed as a dessert?

    a) entrée   b) appetizer   c) mousse   d) culinary

5. Which word applies to the first item that appears on a menu?

    a) appetizer   b) entrée   c) soufflé   d) restaurateur

Circle two words which have either similar or opposite meanings. Write the letter **S** if they are similar, or **O** if they are opposite. *Optional:* Use a thesaurus for more synonyms and antonyms for Exercise A words.

1. gastronomy   indulgence   adulation   worship   _____
2. potable   main course   sautéed   entrée   _____
3. restaurateur   chef   owner   gustatory   _____
4. potable   edible   drinkable   gauche   _____
5. sautéed   raw   culinary   à la carte   _____

J.M.J.

 EXERCISE D   Write on the line the correct list word to complete each sentence.

Mom is a great cook; she probably inherited her __ talents from her mother.	1.
Grandpa allows himself one great __: an afternoon alone fishing on a lake.	2.
After the hurricane, much of the water was no longer __.	3.
Dad likes __ onions and mushrooms with his steak.	4.
Books and magazines on __ are very popular.	5.
That __ owns six eating establishments.	6.
The professor was somewhat embarrassed by the outright __ of his students.	7.
On an __ menu, each item is listed and priced separately.	8.
The success of a restaurant depends greatly on the talent of the __.	9.
An assortment of cheeses and fruit makes a satisfying __ for a meal.	10.
The recipe for this cheese and bacon __ calls for eight eggs!	11.
He was a simple man so he felt somewhat __ at the formal ball.	12.
Even after the substantial __, I had room for dessert.	13.
To satisfy my sweet tooth, I ordered the raspberry __.	14.
The food critic broadened his __ expertise to include French, Italian, and Greek dishes and wines.	15.

51   Vocabulary 8 for Young Catholics   *Jesus, Mary, Joseph, I love You!*

CROSSWORD PUZZLE

Use the words from this lesson to complete the crossword puzzle.

ACROSS

1. relating to cooking
8. owner of a restaurant
9. main dish
11. lacking grace or ease
13. suitable for drinking
14. art of selecting, preparing, and eating food

DOWN

2. food served before a meal and intended to stimulate hunger
3. lightly fried in a small amount of oil or fat
4. light, spongy baked dish made with eggs
5. related to the sense of taste
6. act of doing something for enjoyment or pleasure
7. excessive flattery or admiration
10. light, smooth dessert made with flavored whipped cream and beaten egg whites
12. professional cook

LESSON 14

DESERT DESOLATION (1)

The silent desert extends for miles and miles. Unlike climates with fickle weather, the desert is consistently hot and dry. Vegetation is sparse in this desolate and forsaken land. At first glance, the desert seems to contain only inanimate objects. This deceptive appearance is belied at night, when one can witness the agitation of animals seeking food and water. All creatures that are indigenous to the desert have the inherent ability to conserve water, a vital skill for the successful habitation of this severe land. Whether they are solitary or communal animals, the survival of the stalwart denizens of the desert depends on a balance of instinct, skill, and luck.

(To be continued)

EXERCISE A In the reading above, underline the words (or form of words) that appear in the list below. Based on the meaning in the reading above, write the dictionary definition for the specific part of speech (noun, verb, adjective, adverb, or preposition) as identified in the list.

1. sparse (adj.) _____
2. desolate (adj.) _____
3. forsaken (adj.) _____
4. inanimate (adj.) _____
5. deceptive (adj.) _____
6. belie (v.) _____
7. agitation (n.) _____
8. inherent (adj.) _____
9. habitation (n.) _____
10. indigenous (adj.) _____
11. solitary (adj.) _____
12. communal (adj.) _____
13. stalwart (adj.) _____
14. denizen (n.) _____
15. fickle (adj.) _____

EXERCISE B Circle the correct word.

1. Which word might describe the population of a remote rural village?
   a) indigenous   b) fickle   c) sparse   d) inanimate

2. Which word applies to the lifestyle of a hermit?
   a) communal   b) desolate   c) solitary   d) stalwart

3. Which word may describe both a robot and a rock?
   a) indigenous   b) inanimate   c) inherent   d) forsaken

4. Which word may describe the planet Mars?
   a) desolate   b) deceptive   c) denizen   d) habitation

5. Which word may relate to a kangaroo in Australia but not in Spain?
   a) agitation   b) fickle   c) belie   d) denizen

EXERCISE C Circle two words which have either similar or opposite meanings. Write the letter **S** if they are similar, or **O** if they are opposite. *Optional:* Use a thesaurus for more synonyms and antonyms for Exercise A words.

1. forsaken   fickle   abandoned   deceptive   _____
2. inherent   indigenous   native   solitary   _____
3. habitation   deceive   communal   belie   _____
4. stalwart   inherent   deceptive   fragile   _____
5. fickle   deceptive   true   communal   _____

Write on the line the correct list word to complete each sentence.

The weather is rather ___ here, so be prepared for both sun and rain.	1.
Both Saints Peter and Paul were ___ messengers of the teachings of Christ.	2.
Jesus went to the desert to spend forty days and nights in ___ retreat.	3.
One helpful garden ___ is the earthworm.	4.
Two ___ areas of our planet are the North and South Poles.	5.
In Gethsemane, Jesus felt ___ by His apostles.	6.
Because of the drought, crops were ___ this year.	7.
That island is overgrown with thorny brush, making ___ nearly impossible.	8.
The divinity of Jesus is a belief that is ___ in the Christian faith.	9.
Olives, dates, and figs are products ___ to the Near East.	10.
Priests in religious communities live a ___ lifestyle.	11.
Her smiles ___ the pain in her heart.	12.
It was difficult to distinguish the snail from the ___ objects around it.	13.
The sudden appearance of a field mouse caused some ___ among the students.	14.
That sales pitch is ___ because the product does not do all that!	15.

CROSSWORD PUZZLE

Use the words from this lesson to complete the crossword puzzle.

ACROSS

- **3** inhabitant of a particular place
- **5** bare; meager
- **6** vigorous; outstandingly strong
- **8** native; originating or living naturally in a particular place
- **10** non-living
- **12** state of living or residing in a place
- **14** uninhabited; devoid of living things
- **15** abandoned

DOWN

- **1** implying a false conclusion; misleading
- **2** frenzy; nervous excitement
- **4** shared together, in a group
- **7** existing as an essential part of something
- **9** done or existing alone
- **11** unreliable; capricious; unpredictable; subject to change
- **13** to give a mistaken impression

LESSON 15

DESERT DESOLATION (2)

Closer scrutiny of the desert dispels the aura of quietude that emanates from it. One notes unequivocally frenetic activity that is an intrinsic part of survival for the desert inhabitants. Little creatures clamber up sand hills and scuttle to and from their subterranean abodes. Eyes, antennae and other sensors practically prickle with alertness. Whether furry, scaly, or smooth-skinned, one misstep and predator becomes prey and the pursuer may become a repast. Though generally unobserved, here as elsewhere, the balance of nature is in full play.

EXERCISE A In the reading above, underline the words (or form of words) that appear in the list below. Based on the meaning in the reading above, write the dictionary definition for the specific part of speech (noun, verb, adjective, adverb, or preposition) as identified in the list.

1. dispel (v.) _____
2. aura (n.) _____
3. quietude (n.) _____
4. emanate (v.) _____
5. unequivocally (adv.) _____
6. frenetic (adj.) _____
7. intrinsic (adj.) _____
8. clamber (v.) _____
9. scuttle (v.) _____
10. subterranean (adj.) _____
11. abode (n.) _____
12. prickle (v.) _____
13. misstep (n.) _____
14. predator (n.) _____
15. repast (n.) _____

EXERCISE B Circle the correct word.

1. Which word may relate to a short-legged puppy trying to go up some steps?
   a) scuttle   b) dispel   c) emanate   d) clamber

2. Which word may describe the area where earthworms and ants live?
   a) subterranean   b) frenetic   c) intrinsic   d) prickle

3. Which word applies to a hive for bees and a nest for birds?
   a) quietude   b) predator   c) abode   d) repast

4. Which word may apply to the prayerful atmosphere of a monastery?
   a) emanate   b) aura   c) unequivocally   d) dispel

5. Which word may describe the pace on a street of a large city at rush hour?
   a) misstep   b) prickle   c) scuttle   d) frenetic

EXERCISE C Circle two words which have either similar or opposite meanings. Write the letter **S** if they are similar, or **O** if they are opposite. *Optional:* Use a thesaurus for more synonyms and antonyms for Exercise A words.

1. predator   banquet   abode   repast   _____
2. prickle   stroll   scuttle   emanate   _____
3. scatter   dispel   quietude   intrinsic   _____
4. misstep   predator   prickle   soothe   _____
5. unequivocally undoubtedly   quietude   misstep   _____

EXERCISE D Write on the line the correct list word to complete each sentence.

The angel wanted to __ Mary's fears with reassuring words.	1.
Our Lady __ helped to fulfill the prophecies of the Old Testament.	2.
Sacrificial offerings were an __ part of Jewish rituals.	3.
Mouth-watering aromas __ from that little corner bakery.	4.
One has an immediate sense of __ in the small, simple chapel.	5.
Catacombs are __ resting places for early Roman Christians.	6.
While Mary talked with Jesus, Martha was busy preparing a __ for Him.	7.
The group rehearsed the ceremony so often that they went through it without a single __.	8.
Glen was glad to be at the farm, away from the __ pace of the city.	9.
Our noses __ from the strong aroma of incense.	10.
Soldiers __ out of their trenches to meet the enemy.	11.
A lion is a __, but pandas and deer are not.	12.
Squirrels __ around on the lawn frantically gathering acorns for the winter.	13.
The evening sky over a blanket of snow gives off an __ of peace and security.	14.
I remember my childhood home as a simple __ filled with laughter and children's voices.	15.

CROSSWORD PUZZLE

Use the words from this lesson to complete the crossword puzzle.

ACROSS

1. to make something go away; to do away with
3. tingle
7. energetically fast-paced
8. to issue from a source
10. underground
11. to run in a brisk and hurried manner
13. home; place where one lives
14. particular quality or impression given off by a person, place, or thing
15. error

DOWN

2. essential or natural part of something
4. to climb awkwardly and with difficulty
5. state of stillness; tranquility
6. without doubt; without question
9. animal that lives by hunting and eating other animals
12. meal

LESSON 16

HARMONY IN DIVERSITY

Our family is a motley combination of personalities. The irony is that, rather than pit one person against another, the very disparate nature of the traits tends to balance and complete the group. For example, the more suave and enchanting one assuages the two who are inclined to be more choleric or intense and ameliorates potential conflicts. Our nearly audacious daughter learns moderation from her twin, who tends to be more prudent in thought and action. It has been important for all of us to learn to laugh at ourselves and to be sensitive to one another, and by God's grace, we have managed to do that.

So, my little one, this is what awaits you. It will be fascinating to see how the dynamics will change yet again when you are born into this wonderfully vibrant family!

EXERCISE A — In the reading above, underline the words (or form of words) that appear in the list below. Based on the meaning in the reading above, write the dictionary definition for the specific part of speech (noun, verb, adjective, adverb, or preposition) as identified in the list.

1. motley (adj.) _____
2. irony (n.) _____
3. pit (v.) _____
4. disparate (adj.) _____
5. trait (n.) _____
6. suave (adj.) _____
7. enchanting (adj.) _____
8. assuage (v.) _____
9. choleric (adj.) _____
10. intense (adj.) _____
11. ameliorate (v.) _____
12. audacious (adj.) _____
13. moderation (n.) _____
14. prudent (adj.) _____
15. dynamics (n.) _____

EXERCISE B Circle the correct word.

1. Which word may describe someone who quickly loses his temper?
   a) choleric   b) intense   c) audacious   d) disparate

2. Which word may describe a serious person who does not tend to smile easily?
   a) audacious   b) intense   c) prudent   d) suave

3. Which word would likely describe a grouping of people chosen at random?
   a) choleric   b) audacious   c) suave   d) motley

4. Which word may relate to the role of a referee or an arbitrator?
   a) pit   b) trait   c) ameliorate   d) dynamics

5. Which word may apply to the surprising twist in a story?
   a) ameliorate   b) assuage   c) irony   d) trait

EXERCISE C Circle two words which have either similar or opposite meanings. Write the letter **S** if they are similar, or **O** if they are opposite. *Optional:* Use a thesaurus for more synonyms and antonyms for Exercise A words.

1. irony   excess   trait   moderation   _____
2. intense   prudent   coarse   suave   _____
3. disparate   bold   audacious   enchanting   _____
4. enchanting   charming   trait   assuage   _____
5. disparate   dynamics   identical   assuage   _____

EXERCISE D Write on the line the correct list word to complete each sentence.

It is important to be __ in our choice of friends.	1.
The Garden of Eden was a truly __ place.	2.
Omniscience is a __ possessed only by God.	3.
Mom's soothing voice and tender touch __ the crying baby.	4.
The mayor's voice of reason served to __ the tension in the council chamber.	5.
Pharisees tried to __ the people against Jesus by challenging His teachings.	6.
The __ in the Parable of the Prodigal Son is the utmost forgiveness the father shows his repentant son.	7.
His look is so __, he seems to see right through you.	8.
The captain's __ disposition often puts the rest of the men in a bad mood.	9.
The __ manner of the main character makes him likeable from the very beginning of the play.	10.
Wise religious teachers have always advocated __ in all things.	11.
New York in the 19th century was inhabited by people of several __ cultures.	12.
Of all the apostles, St. Peter is clearly the most __.	13.
A sudden shift in the jet stream may affect the entire __ of a weather system.	14.
Our Lord chose a rather __ group of men to be His apostles.	15.

CROSSWORD PUZZLE

Use the words from this lesson to complete the crossword puzzle.

ACROSS

1. cautious; careful
7. impatient and quickly irritated
12. the different forces that affect changes in a system
13. to set someone or something against another
14. to make a situation more agreeable or tolerable
15. having a number of unlike parts or characteristics

DOWN

2. distinguishing characteristic
3. fearless; tending to take bold risks
4. avoidance of excess; easing of a condition
5. inconsistency between an expected and an actual result
6. having the ability to charm or attract
8. essentially different; separate and unique
9. to ease; to soothe
10. smooth; agreeable
11. very serious or earnest

LESSON 17

THE RUNAWAY

Our neighbor pounded on our door and shouted, "Come! Quick! Sadie is on the loose!" Those words conjured images ranging from disruption, to pandemonium, to devastation. You see, Sadie is our docile but intrepid St. Bernard.

"But we were just watching her frolic in the piles of leaves! What could have gotten into her?"

We stepped outdoors, took a whiff of hamburgers sizzling on a nearby grill, and instantly had our answer. Clearly, Sadie had executed a high leap over our fence and galloped headlong to the source of the irresistible aroma.

We flew up the street and soon spotted the interloper as our neighbor served her a hamburger which Sadie obviously considered most delectable. After a profusion of apologies made to and accepted by our friends, we shared a good laugh. We tethered Sadie on a short leash, and went home relieved that we had found her and that we had not lost any friends over her antics.

Of all the anecdotes of our Sadie's escapades, this is our favorite.

EXERCISE A In the reading above, underline the words (or form of words) that appear in the list below. Based on the meaning in the reading above, write the dictionary definition for the specific part of speech (noun, verb, adjective, adverb, or preposition) as identified in the list.

1. conjure (v.) _____
2. disruption (n.) _____
3. pandemonium (n.) _____
4. devastation (n.) _____
5. docile (adj.) _____
6. intrepid (adj.) _____
7. frolic (v.) _____
8. whiff (n.) _____
9. execute (v.) _____
10. irresistible (adj.) _____
11. interloper (n.) _____
12. profusion (n.) _____
13. tether (v.) _____
14. anecdote (n.) _____
15. escapade (n.) _____

EXERCISE B Circle the correct word.

1. Which word relates to a child who rarely needs a reprimand?
   a) intrepid   b) irresistible   c) docile   d) disruption

2. Which word relates to children playing games on a beach?
   a) conjure   b) frolic   c) interloper   d) escapade

3. Which word may apply to stories adults may tell about their younger days?
   a) anecdote   b) conjure   c) profusion   d) pandemonium

4. Which word may apply when a fire alarm sounds off during a town council meeting?
   a) devastation   b) disruption   c) whiff   d) tether

5. Which word relates to securing a boat to a dock?
   a) execute   b) conjure   c) intrepid   d) tether

EXERCISE C Circle two words which have either similar or opposite meanings. Write the letter **S** if they are similar, or **O** if they are opposite. **Optional:** Use a thesaurus for more synonyms and antonyms for Exercise A words.

1. pandemonium   bold   profusion   intrepid   _____
2. escapade   devastation   profusion   scarcity   _____
3. execute   complete   conjure   interloper   _____
4. frenzy   devastation   escapade   pandemonium   _____
5. conjure   guest   interloper   escapade   _____

Write on the line the correct list word to complete each sentence.

There was __ in Egypt after God sent plagues to punish Pharaoh.	1.
We were delighted to watch fawns __ in the meadow.	2.
The blind man felt a __ of gratitude when Jesus healed him.	3.
The ranch hand showed us how to __ our horses so they would not stray.	4.
On a hot day a tall glass of cold lemonade is __.	5.
The aromas emerging from Mom's kitchen __ images of Christmas cookies.	6.
A __ of beef stew simmering made our stomachs rumble.	7.
Our Lord was __ as a lamb as He was led to Golgotha to fulfill the will of His Father.	8.
When an elephant's young is threatened, she becomes __ in the face of danger.	9.
Father Murphy often uses an __ to make a point.	10.
Herod told his men to __ his order to kill all male babies under two years old.	11.
The startled horse caused a __ in the Memorial Day parade.	12.
Uncle Robert led many an __ during his years with the rodeo.	13.
Word that a gorilla had escaped led to __ among the visitors at the zoo.	14.
The uninvited stranger was an __ at our Christmas party.	15.

CROSSWORD PUZZLE

Use the words from this lesson to complete the crossword puzzle.

ACROSS

3 to perform; to complete a skillful act or maneuver
5 an event involving mischief or excitement
9 person who interferes where he does not belong
10 impossible to turn down
11 to call to mind; to produce unexpectedly
12 wild, noisy confusion and disorder
13 disturbance or disorder caused by an interruption
14 ruin; destruction; total damage

DOWN

1 to tie or fasten as with a rope to restrict movement
2 easily trained or managed; submissive
4 to play energetically and happily
6 plentiful quantity or amount; abundance; exuberance
7 a short account of an interesting or funny incident
8 quick puff of air; quick sniff of an aroma
10 having no fear

LESSON 18

WHATEVER FLOATS YOUR BOAT (1)

The Fourth of July picnic with its "Float Your Boat" contest is imminent. The contest gives people the opportunity to flat out flout--or even try to redefine--the laws of physics. You see, the object is to make a floating device from scratch using only recycled material. The hypothesis is this: it is feasible to construct a buoyant vessel from scraps of junk.

It's the same every summer. For weeks, men and women, boys and girls ransack garages, sheds, and junk yards. They scour flea markets and yard sales to scavenge for suitable parts. With unrestrained ardor, they gather a miscellany of objects that just might comprise the exact apparatus that will make a contraption that floats. Then, dauntless, and usually equipped with much more optimism than skill, they put together their "boats."   *(To be continued)*

EXERCISE A In the reading above, underline the words (or form of words) that appear in the list below. Based on the meaning in the reading above, write the dictionary definition for the specific part of speech (noun, verb, adjective, adverb, or preposition) as identified in the list.

1. flout (v.) _____
2. physics (n.) _____
3. hypothesis (n.) _____
4. feasible (adj.) _____
5. buoyant (adj.) _____
6. ransack (v.) _____
7. scour (v.) _____
8. scavenge (v.) _____
9. ardor (n.) _____
10. miscellany (n.) _____
11. comprise (v.) _____
12. apparatus (n.) _____
13. contraption (n.) _____
14. dauntless (adj.) _____
15. optimism (n.) _____

J.M.J.

EXERCISE B Circle the correct word.

1. Which word relates to the strong feelings one might have about a special cause?
   a) hypothesis   b) ardor   c) apparatus   d) miscellany

2. Which word relates to the items that are required to conduct a scientific experiment?
   a) physics   b) contraption   c) apparatus   d) miscellany

3. Which word may apply to an invention that is put together with items one might find about the house?
   a) contraption   b) ransack   c) scavenge   d) comprise

4. Which word may apply when we look desperately through drawers and closets to find a lost bracelet?
   a) buoyant   b) scavenge   c) comprise   d) ransack

5. Which word might suggest the possibility of success?
   a) buoyant   b) comprise   c) dauntless   d) feasible

EXERCISE C Circle two words which have either similar or opposite meanings. Write the letter **S** if they are similar, or **O** if they are opposite. *Optional:* Use a thesaurus for more synonyms and antonyms for Exercise A words.

1. buoyant   optimism   feasible   doubt   _____
2. miscellany   sets   contraption   physics   _____
3. scour   comprise   flout   comply   _____
4. physics   hypothesis   scavenge   fact   _____
5. buoyant   dauntless   determined   scour   _____

Jesus, Mary, Joseph, I love You!

EXERCISE D Write on the line the correct list word to complete each sentence.

When Paul was Saul, he was __ in his efforts to persecute Christians.	1.
The rich young man did not __ any of the Jewish laws; indeed, he embraced them.	2.
The disciples did not think it was __ to feed the crowd with five loaves and two fishes.	3.
Noah followed God's instructions, and the huge ark became __ in the flood.	4.
Thomas Edison applied his knowledge of __ to invent machines that could record and play sounds.	5.
Our refrigerator door displays a __ of items such as pictures, notes, and keys.	6.
With deep __, Mom practices a special devotion to the Sacred Heart.	7.
Several solar systems and galaxies __ the vast universe.	8.
In the evenings, sea gulls swoop down on trash barrels to __ for food.	9.
Armed with her photography __, Aunt Harriet sets off to the mountains.	10.
When we go to the park, we __ the area for the perfect picnic spot.	11.
Grandma insists that a heart filled with __ greatly contributes to one's general good health.	12.
Our agriculture museum displays one __ after another that demonstrates the cleverness of early farmers.	13.
A scientist tests a __ several times to ensure that it is correct.	14.
The Gestapo would __ people's homes for evidence that they were hiding Jews.	15.

CROSSWORD PUZZLE

Use the words from this lesson to complete the crossword puzzle.

ACROSS

2 branch of science that addresses the properties of matter and energy and how they work together
4 able or likely to stay afloat
8 confidence that everything will be all right
10 possible, easy, or convenient to do
11 determined; not subject to discouragement or fear of failure
14 to disregard dismissively; to blatantly ignore
15 to collect from discarded items anything that is usable

DOWN

1 assumption; possible but unproven guess that something is true
3 complicated or strange-looking device that is usually crudely made
5 materials or items used for a particular purpose
6 to make up or form; to consist of
7 a collection or mixture of unlike items
9 to search thoroughly
12 eagerness; enthusiasm; passion
13 to search rapidly over a wide area

LESSON 19

WHATEVER FLOATS YOUR BOAT (2)

On the morning of July 4, a bevy of would-be mariners convenes at the lake. What bedlam is caused by this hodgepodge of animated people and the cumbersome crafts they lug with them! As they shove-off into the water, bystanders get a good look at this year's entries. In appearance, they vary from homely to garish. Structurally, they range from the precarious to the promising.

A close look at some of the components leads one to question their utility. While a few pieces are recognizable -- the gears and pedals of a bicycle, a washing machine motor, and a stovepipe, for example -- the identity of other parts and devices is more obscure. What is that appendage poking out the top, or that one that is bulging from the sides?

Well, inevitably, one by one, the boats succumb to gravity. There is a winner, though, and it will be proudly displayed on the Float Your Boat float in the parade this afternoon!

As for the others, well, there is always next year!

EXERCISE A In the reading above, underline the words (or form of words) that appear in the list below. Based on the meaning in the reading above, write the dictionary definition for the specific part of speech (noun, verb, adjective, adverb, or preposition) as identified in the list.

1. bevy (n.) _____
2. would-be (adj.) _____
3. mariner (n.) _____
4. convene (v.) _____
5. bedlam (n.) _____
6. hodgepodge (n.) _____
7. cumbersome (adj.) _____
8. lug (v.) _____
9. homely (adj.) _____
10. garish (adj.) _____
11. precarious (adj.) _____
12. utility (n.) _____
13. device (n.) _____
14. obscure (adj.) _____
15. appendage (n.) _____

EXERCISE B — Circle the correct word.

1. Which word may apply to a dog's tail?
   a) obscure   b) garish   c) utility   d) appendage

2. Which word may apply to someone who works hard at becoming an actor?
   a) precarious   b) cumbersome   c) would-be   d) device

3. Which word may describe luggage one carries through an airport?
   a) cumbersome   b) obscure   c) device   d) utility

4. Which word may relate to pigeons near a popcorn stand?
   a) hodgepodge   b) bevy   c) lug   d) promising

5. Which word may relate to the helpfulness of a gadget?
   a) device   b) precarious   c) utility   d) homely

EXERCISE C — Circle two words which have either similar or opposite meanings. Write the letter **S** if they are similar, or **O** if they are opposite. *Optional:* Use a thesaurus for more synonyms and antonyms for Exercise A words.

1. homely   would-be   garish   mariner   _____
2. precarious   convene   lug   invincible   _____
3. device   obscure   hodgepodge   unclear   _____
4. showy   frenzy   convene   bedlam   _____
5. mariner   bevy   hodgepodge   miscellany   _____

EXERCISE D Write on the line the correct list word to complete each sentence.

Cardinals ___ in Rome to elect a pope.	1.
There was complete ___ before the Tower of Babel was completed.	2.
The homes of the simple folk of Nazareth were ___ and airy.	3.
A ___ of women gathered at the river on laundry day.	4.
The ___ prayed to his patron, St. Peter Gonzales.	5.
Almost everyone in this country owns some sort of electronic ___.	6.
The nets were so full of fish, it took several men to ___ them into the boat.	7.
An insignificant bread crumb can be a ___ load for an ant.	8.
For a butterfly, the antenna is an essential ___.	9.
Frank, a ___ artist, bought paints, brushes, and canvases.	10.
Some of today's renowned artists were ___ while they were alive.	11.
Noah's neighbors ridiculed him and questioned the ___ of his huge ark.	12.
Circus performers usually wear ___ costumes for their acts.	13.
A flea market offers a ___ of items at low prices.	14.
An agreement made between untrustworthy foes is ___ indeed.	15.

CROSSWORD PUZZLE

Use the words from this lesson to complete the crossword puzzle.

ACROSS

2 simple and plain-looking
7 piece of equipment meant for a particular purpose
8 to pull or to carry with difficulty
10 large group
12 dangerously unsteady; subject to collapse
13 to gather together as a group
14 scene of commotion and confusion

DOWN

1 aspiring; intending; wishful
2 jumble; confused mixture
3 usefulness; state of being beneficial
4 showy; gaudy
5 something that is added or attached to a larger main object
6 difficult to maneuver because of size or weight
9 sailor
11 not readily apparent

LESSON 20

THE STORYTELLER

Storytelling is an art. To merely recount details or to deliver a stilted narration of events is not storytelling. Rather, those who are gifted with this talent have an innate aptitude for manipulating voice intonation and cadence and their facial expressions for maximum effect. With equal skill, they can relate a convincingly eerie ghost story and an uproarious tale of someone's eventful yet benign misadventures. Further, the storyteller who replicates sounds or who mimics dialects or mannerisms will, without fail, enthrall an audience.

Often in a particular area, a storyteller emerges who can regale others with stories full of folklore with which whole audiences can readily identify. Start practicing now and maybe someday you will be that storyteller.

EXERCISE A In the reading above, underline the words (or form of words) that appear in the list below. Based on the meaning in the reading above, write the dictionary definition for the specific part of speech (noun, verb, adjective, adverb, or preposition) as identified in the list.

1. recount (v.) _____
2. stilted (adj.) _____
3. innate (adj.) _____
4. intonation (n.) _____
5. cadence (n.) _____
6. eerie (adj.) _____
7. uproarious (adj.) _____
8. benign (adj.) _____
9. misadventure (n.) _____
10. dialect (n.) _____
11. mannerism (n.) _____
12. enthrall (v.) _____
13. regale (v.) _____
14. folklore (n.) _____
15. identify (v.) _____

J.M.J.

EXERCISE B Circle the correct word.

1. Which word applies when an entertainer captures the full attention of the audience?
   a) innate   b) recount   c) enthrall   d) identify

2. Which word may describe noticeably windy conditions that do not cause any damage?
   a) stilted   b) eerie   c) uproarious   d) benign

3. Which word may relate to the characteristic speech known as the "southern drawl"?
   a) dialect   b) mannerism   c) folklore   d) cadence

4. Which word may apply when a person can relate to someone else's experience?
   a) recount   b) identify   c) regale   d) innate

5. Which word may apply when witnesses give details of an accident?
   a) stilted   b) eerie   c) recount   d) intonation

EXERCISE C Circle two words which have either similar or opposite meanings. Write the letter **S** if they are similar, or **O** if they are opposite. *Optional:* Use a thesaurus for more synonyms and antonyms for Exercise A words.

1. eerie   stilted   innate   rigid   _____
2. intonation   mannerism   eerie   reassuring   _____
3. misadventure   folklore   mannerism   accident   _____
4. intonation   cadence   rhythm   regale   _____
5. regale   intonation   amuse   mannerism   _____

Exercise D Write on the line the correct list word to complete each sentence.

We listened to my aunt ___ the highlights of her trip to the Holy Land.	1.
The Gospel singer knew how to ___ the crowds with his singing.	2.
The story that Grandfather told us is considered German ___.	3.
The brothers in that family engage in some ___teasing.	4.
Dolores was so nervous that she gave a rather ___ presentation.	5.
Helen gave ___ accounts of the antics of her mischievous brothers.	6.
We recognized his Cajun ___ as soon as he started to speak.	7.
As a music student, Rita can ___ with Lucy's love of Mozart.	8.
The drums matched the ___ of the marching soldiers' footsteps.	9.
When Our Lord died, the skies darkened, giving the site an ___ appearance.	10.
Our Lady had an ___ desire to fulfill God's will.	11.
Effective lectors read the Mass readings with just the right voice ___.	12.
Our uncle is so accident-prone that his life is one ___ after another!	13.
The lieutenant's confident ___ was reassuring to the troops.	14.
The talented puppeteers never fail to ___ the children with each performance.	15.

79 Vocabulary 8 for Young Catholics

CROSSWORD PUZZLE

Use the words from this lesson to complete the crossword puzzle.

ACROSS

4 stories and traditions held by certain groups and passed on through generations
7 language that is characteristic of a particular region; words and expressions used by people of a given area
12 the rise and fall of the voice in speech
14 rhythm; tempo; the beat of sounds
15 mild; harmless

DOWN

1 to entertain tremendously
2 unfortunate incident
3 to tell in detail; to give an account of an event or experience
5 to fascinate; to capture another's full attention
6 to regard oneself as having some of the same characteristics as another
8 unnaturally stiff
9 hilarious; extremely funny
10 characteristic ways of acting
11 inborn; in one's nature
13 causing uneasiness or fear

Glossary

bland – plain; unlikely to be noticed

a la carte – having dishes on a menu listed separately and individually priced

abode – home; place where one lives

accuracy – correctness; precision

address – to speak to directly

adhesive – able to stick; gluey; clingy

adjacent – next to; beside

adroit – skillful with one's hands; very able

adulation – excessive flattery or admiration; overenthusiastic praise

affable – friendly; good-natured; easy-going around people; sociable

agitation – frenzy; nervous excitement; turmoil

allude – to refer to without actually naming; to suggest

alms – money for the poor; anything given as charity

altimeter – instrument used to measure height or altitude

ambivalence – mixed or contradictory feelings

ameliorate – to make a situation more agreeable or tolerable; alleviate

amorphous – having no clearly defined shape; formless

anecdote – a short account of an interesting or funny incident

anticipate – to foresee and plan for ahead of time; to expect

apathy – lack of feeling or concern; uncaring attitude

apparatus – materials or items used for a particular purpose

appendage – something that is added or attached to a larger main object

appetizer – food served before a meal and intended to stimulate hunger

ardor – eagerness; enthusiasm; passion

array – certain order or arrangement of items; collection

ascertain – to make sure; to find out for certain

assemble – to fit parts together to form a whole

assortment – variety; collection of different items

assuage – to ease; to soothe; make less severe

audacious – fearless; tending to take bold risks; daring

aura – particular quality or impression given off by a person, place, or thing; mood

autobiography – a person's written account of his own life

autograph – a person's name handwritten by himself; one's own signature

banal – unoriginal; ordinary

bedlam – scene of commotion and confusion

begrudgingly – in a resentfully reluctant manner; with envy

behavior – the way one acts or conducts himself; conduct

belie – to give a mistaken impression; contradict

benign – mild; harmless

bevy – large group

biology – study of living things

blatant – very obvious

blemish – imperfection; flaw

blunder – careless mistake; mistake due to lack of thought, insight, or knowledge

bridal – related to a bride or a wedding

bridle – part of the harness that fits over the head of a horse

brogue – manner of speaking characteristic of the Irish

buoyant – able or likely to stay afloat

bustle – to move about in an energetic or noisy manner; to hurry excitedly

cadence – rhythm; tempo; the beat of sounds

captivate – to charm; to win someone over

capture – to catch; grab

changeable – likely to become different suddenly

chef – professional cook

choleric – impatient and quickly irritated

clamber – to climb awkwardly and with difficulty

cliché – word or phrase that becomes stale from overuse

collaborate – to work jointly on a project or activity; cooperate

colossal – extremely large; huge

commonplace – usual; ordinary; undistinguished and uninteresting

communal – shared together, in a group

compel – to force or to pressure someone to do something

complement – to complete or to make perfect

compliment – to express praise or admiration or approval

component – part of a larger whole; ingredient

comprise – to make up or form; to consist of

confounded – confused; perplexed; bewildered

conjure – to call to mind; to produce unexpectedly

consider – to think carefully about; evaluate

conspicuous – attracting attention; obvious

consternation – dismay; feeling of helplessness; anxiety; confusion

contraption – complicated or strange-looking device that is usually crudely made; gadget

convene – to gather together as a group; to assemble

conversely – in reversed order

course – direction; route

creativity – originality; inventiveness

cringe – to shrink in fear; shudder

cryptograph – something written in code

culinary – relating to cooking; style or quality of cooking

cumbersome – difficult to maneuver because of size or weight

curio – object that is rare or interesting or unusual

dauntless – determined; not subject to discouragement or fear of failure

dearth – small supply; scarcity; shortage

deceptive – implying a false conclusion; misleading; dishonest

decipher – to decode; to figure out the meaning

deftly – in a skillful manner; cleverly

degenerate – having lost any desirable qualities; having deteriorated

degrading – humiliating; causing lack of self-respect; cheapening

delectable – delicious; highly pleasing

delete – to eliminate; to remove

denizen – inhabitant of a particular place; resident

desolate – uninhabited; devoid of living things; dreary

devastation – ruin or destruction; total damage

device – piece of equipment meant for a particular purpose; a tool

devoid – lacking; empty

dialect – language that is characteristic of a particular region; words and expressions used by people of a given area

dilemma – situation that requires a difficult choice between two or more things

discern – to distinguish; to tell the difference

dismantle – to take apart

disparate – essentially different; separate and unique; dissimilar

dispel – to make something go away; to do away with; to cause to vanish

disruption – disturbance or disorder caused by an interruption

dissipate – to disappear gradually to vanishing; to dissolve

diverge – to move away from a common point; go in different directions

divulge – to reveal; to make known

docile – easily trained or managed; submissive

dubious – questionable; uncertain

dynamics – the different forces that affect changes in a system

eerie – causing uneasiness or fear; strange

elude – to escape one's grasp or understanding; avoid

emanate – to issue from a source; originate

enchanting – having the ability to charm or attract; fascinating

enhance – to improve; to increase the quality of something

enthrall – to fascinate; to capture another's full attention

entreat – to ask for earnestly; to beg or plead; to petition

entrée – main dish of a meal

erroneous – incorrect; wrong

escapade – an event involving mischief or excitement; a wild prank

execute – to perform; to complete a skillful act or maneuver; to accomplish

exotic – unusual; out of the ordinary

exuberance – excitement; lively energy

fad – short-lived widely held enthusiasm over some practice or interest; temporary fashion

fathom – to comprehend something strange or puzzling; figure out

feasible – possible, easy, or convenient to do

fickle – unreliable; capricious; unpredictable; subject to change

flat – British term for apartment

flout – to disregard dismissively; to blatantly ignore; to mock

folklore – stories and traditions held by certain groups and passed on through generations

forsaken – abandoned; deserted

frenetic – energetically fast-paced; in a panic

frolic – to play energetically and happily; romp

fulfill – to live up to; to bring to reality something that is promised or understood

garish – showy; gaudy

garland – rope or string of items such as flowers, fruit or leaves

gastronomy – art of selecting, preparing, and eating food; culinary science

gauche – lacking grace or ease; awkward

geology – study of the earth's structure

graphology – study of handwriting

grapple – to wrestle; to grasp and struggle with; to grab

grip – to hold firmly; to grasp

guile – trickery; dishonesty; deceit

gustatory – relating to the sense of taste

habitation – state of living or residing in a place

hodgepodge – jumble; confused mixture

homely – simple and plain-looking

humble – modest; simple; meek

humdrum – lacking excitement; boring

hunker – to crouch; to settle in for awhile; squat

hyperventilate – to breathe at an unnaturally fast rate

hypothesis – assumption; possible but unproven guess that something is true

identify – to regard oneself as having some of the same characteristics as another; confirm

impish – mischievous; tricky in a playful way

imply – to suggest as fact something that is not actually stated

inanimate – non-living; lifeless

incidence – rate or frequency of occurrence; episode

incident – event; occurrence

inclination – tendency; a leaning toward a particular thought or action

indefatigably – untiringly; tirelessly; energetically

indelibly – in a manner that is impossible to remove or erase; permanently

indigenous – native; originating or living naturally in a particular place; inherent

indignant – feeling anger at what seems undeserved treatment; expressing strong displeasure

indulgence – act of doing something for enjoyment or pleasure; gratification

inherent – existing as an essential part of something; basic; inborn

innate – inborn; in one's nature

insolent – showing rudeness and lack of respect

insomnia – sleeplessness

intense – very serious or earnest; profound

interject – to place or include among other things

interloper – person who interferes where he does not belong; a meddler

intonation – the rise and fall of the voice in speech

intrepid – having no fear; bold

intrinsic – essential or natural part of something; basic; hereditary

invaluable – of great worth; priceless

inviting – appealing; attractive

irony – inconsistency between an expected and an actual result; sarcasm

irresistible – impossible to turn down; tempting

jostle – to push, elbow, or bump against, usually in a crowd

kale – variety of cabbage

lavish – extravagant; elaborate

lug – to pull or to carry with difficulty

maintain – to strongly state to be true or factual; to insist

maneuver – to move skillfully to attain a goal

mannerism – characteristic ways of acting

mariner – sailor

maze – complicated network of paths; a puzzle

mesmerize – to make spellbound; to transfix; to hypnotize

mien – manner; conduct; behavior

misadventure – unfortunate incident

miscellany – a collection or mixture of unlike items

misnomer – incorrect or inaccurate name or designation; an error in naming a person or thing

misstep – error

misuse – to use the wrong way or for the wrong purpose;

moderation – avoidance of excess; easing of a condition

motley – having a number of unlike parts or characteristics; varied; mixed

mousse – light, smooth dessert made with flavored whipped cream

nape – the back of the neck

nondescript – having no distinctive characteristics; uninteresting and dull

noted – well-known and respected; esteemed

notorious – well-known in an unfavorable way; dishonorable

obscure – not readily apparent; unclear

omit – to leave out; to neglect

optimism – confidence that everything will be all right; state of having positive beliefs

originate – to come from; to arise from a source

outright – complete; absolute; total

overwhelm – to overpower; bewilder

oxymoron – a self-contradictory expression; figure of speech not meant literally

paltry – of little importance or value; trivial

panacea – cure for any disease; solution for all problems; a cure-all

pandemic – disease that spreads throughout a wide area; a wide-spread plague

pandemonium – wild, noisy confusion and disorder; utter chaos

papaya – elongated, edible tropical fruit that contains many black seeds

pauper – very poor person; a beggar

perimeter – the length of a line that forms a boundary; borderline

photocopy – duplicate of written or printed material produced by the action of light on a specially prepared surface

physics – branch of science that addresses the properties of matter and energy and how they work together

pit – to set someone or something against another

pitfall – trap; snare; threat

potable – suitable for drinking; drinkable

precarious – dangerously unsteady; subject to collapse; hazardous

predator – animal that lives by hunting and eating other animals

premeditate – to think about and plan carefully ahead of time; to consider beforehand

pretentious – trying to appear more important than one actually is; conceited; snobbish

prevalent – widespread; extensive

prickle – tingle; to cause a tingling sensation

principal – main; of greatest importance

principle – basic truth; rule or belief that governs one's behavior

produce – fresh fruit and vegetables

profusion – plentiful quantity or amount; abundance; exuberance

prompt – to cause to do something; to motivate

prudent – cautious; careful; wise

quietude – state of stillness; tranquility; calmness

quirk – an odd habit or characteristic; whim

ragamuffin – poorly clothed child

rankle – to annoy; to irritate

ransack – to search thoroughly; plunder

recount – to tell in detail; to give an account of an event or experience

redundancy – the use of unnecessary words; overabundance

regale – to entertain tremendously

relinquish – to give up or give over; to let go

repast – meal

repetitive – marked by being stated or said again; continual

replica – copy; duplicate of an original

requisite – necessary for achieving a particular goal or purpose; essential

resolute – determined; unwavering

respectively – in the order given; correspondingly

restaurateur – owner of a restaurant

retrieve – to take back; to regain possession of

rogue – dishonest or tricky person; person without principles

rue – regret; to feel sorrow for

sauteed – lightly cooked or browned in a small amount of oil or fat

scavenge – to collect from discarded items anything that is usable

scornfully – with contempt or disdain

scour – to search rapidly over a wide area

scruffy – untidy and shabby; messy

scuttle – to run in a brisk and hurried manner; to move around quickly

secondary – of lesser importance

seismograph – instrument used to measure vibrations of the earth

sneer – scornful smile that shows contempt

solitary – done or existing alone; single; isolated

souffle – light, spongy baked dish made with eggs

sparse – bare; meager

stalwart – vigorous; outstandingly strong; valiant; fearless

standstill – condition in which there is no movement or activity; halt

stature – a person's height; height of any object

stilted – unnaturally stiff; constrained

stoke – to stir up; to kindle

straightforward – uncomplicated; clear; honest; direct

stupefy – to bewilder; to perplex

suave – smooth; agreeable; sophisticated in manner or attitude

subterranean – underground

subtle – difficult to distinguish; delicate and mysterious

successive – one after another; following

succinct – concise; short and to the point

sundry – various; mixed selection

superfluous – extra; unnecessary; excessive

survey – to look at carefully and in an investigative way; examine; evaluate

susceptible – likely to give in to an action; having no resistance

tether – to tie or fasten as with a rope to restrict movement

throng – crowd; large, packed number of people; a multitude

thunderstruck – stunned; shocked

timidly – with shyness; fearfully

timorously – in a shy and fearful manner; nervously

touching – causing feelings of sympathy or tenderness; affecting

touchy – overly sensitive; easily hurt

trait – distinguishing characteristic; disposition

transit – carrying of persons or goods from one place to another; passage

unavoidable – unable to be prevented; certain

uncanny – eerie; mysterious

understated – expressed or done in a simple way; lessened the importance of

unequivocally – without doubt; without question; certainly

unexpected – not seen as likely to happen; not foreseen; sudden

unsightly – ugly; frightful

uproarious – hilarious; extremely funny

utility – usefulness; state of being beneficial

vacillate – to waver between one choice and another; to be indecisive

veer – to change direction suddenly

veritable – true; actual; authentic

vernacular – ordinary language; common or usual speech

whiff – quick puff or air; quick sniff of an aroma

would-be – aspiring; intending; wishful

Answer Key

Lesson 1

Ex. B
1. d) succinct
2. a) conversely
3. b) creativity
4. c) insomnia
5. c) humdrum

Ex. C
1. S attractive, inviting
2. S grip, grasp
3. O outright, somewhat
4. S improve, enhance
5. S charm, captivate

Ex. D
1. inviting
2. succinct
3. outright
4. insomnia
5. thunderstruck
6. conversely
7. bland
8. captivate
9. secondary
10. mesmerize
11. grip
12. enhance
13. capture
14. humdrum
15. creativity

Crossword Puzzle

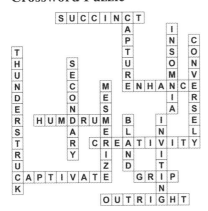

Lesson 2

Ex. B
1. a) conspicuous
2. b) sundry
3. d) curio
4. c) discern
5. b) adjacent

Ex. C
1. O dubious, certain
2. O replica, original
3. S unsightly, ugly
4. O worthless, invaluable
5. S dearth, scarcity

Ex. D
1. uncanny
2. discern
3. unsightly
4. blemish
5. relinquish
6. conspicuous
7. dearth
8. paltry
9. devoid
10. replica
11. adjacent
12. sundry
13. curio
14. dubious
15. invaluable

Crossword Puzzle

Lesson 3

Ex. B
1. c) veer
2. b) fulfill
3. a) course
4. d) imply
5. c) anticipate

Ex. C
1. S behavior, action
2. O compel, suggest
3. O changeable, predictable
4. S unexpected, unforeseen
5. S inclination, tendency

Ex. D
1. veer
2. inclination
3. course
4. diverge
5. anticipate
6. behavior
7. changeable
8. compel
9. fulfill
10. susceptible
11. unexpected
12. stupefy
13. imply
14. unavoidable
15. quirk

Crossword Puzzle

Lesson 4

Ex. B
1. d) maneuver
2. b) indelibly
3. a) throng
4. c) assortment
5. b) jostle

Ex. C
1. O banal, exotic
2. O colossal, miniscule
3. S maze, puzzle
4. S delectable, tasty
5. S rush, bustle

Ex. D
1. papaya
2. garland
3. exotic
4. bustle
5. colossal
6. throng
7. maze
8. overwhelm
9. maneuver
10. jostle
11. produce
12. assortment
13. delectable
14. banal
15. indelibly

Crossword Puzzle

Lesson 5

Ex. B

1. a) impish
2. b) deftly
3. c) premeditate
4. d) affable
5. b) array

Ex. C

1. O divulge, hide
2. S study, survey
3. S prompt, urge
4. O understated, lavish
5. O stoke, extinguish

Ex. D

1. divulge
2. affable
3. brogue
4. prompt
5. decipher
6. stoke
7. survey
8. lavish
9. deftly
10. impish
11. kale
12. mien
13. array
14. understated
15. premeditate

Crossword Puzzle

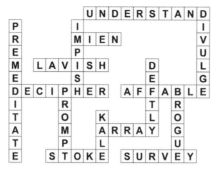

Lesson 6

Ex. B

1. d) touching
2. c) successive
3. a) notorious
4. b) principle
5. c) compliment

Ex. C

1. S bridle, harness
2. O noted, unknown
3. O principal, insignificant
4. S allude, suggest
5. S happening, incident

Ex. D

1. bridal
2. compliment
3. complement
4. notorious
5. incident
6. elude
7. principle
8. incidence
9. successive
10. noted
11. principal
12. touching
13. touchy
14. allude
15. bridle

Crossword Puzzle

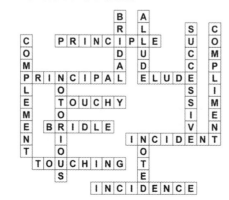

Lesson 7

Ex. B

1. c) adroit
2. b) indefatigably
3. a) dissipate
4. d) straightforward
5. b) rankle

Ex. C

1. O consternation, exuberance
2. O assemble, dismantle
3. O include, omit
4. S begrudgingly, reluctantly
5. O requisite, optional

Ex. D

1. resolute
2. omit
3. ascertain
4. exuberance
5. rankle
6. dissipate
7. straightforward
8. begrudgingly
9. indefatigably
10. requisite
11. component
12. dismantle
13. adroit
14. assemble
15. consternation

Crossword Puzzle

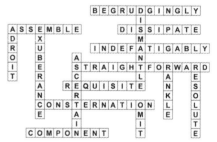

Lesson 8

Ex. B

1. a) rue
2. c) vernacular
3. c) erroneous
4. d) standstill
5. a) blunder

Ex. C

1. O subtle, blatant
2. S oxymoron, contradiction
3. O unusual, commonplace
4. O transit, standstill
5. S duplicate, photocopy

Ex. D

1. misuse
2. accuracy
3. oxymoron
4. erroneous
5. blatant
6. standstill
7. vernacular
8. photocopy
9. subtle
10. blunder
11. transit
12. misnomer
13. commonplace
14. rue
15. adhesive

Crossword Puzzle

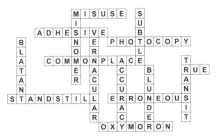

Lesson 9

Ex. B

1. d) superfluous
2. d) collaborate
3. b) pitfall
4. a) vacillate
5. c) prevalent

Ex. C

1. O interject, omit
2. S delete, erase
3. O consider, dismiss
4. S redundancy, repetition
5. S fad, craze

Ex. D

1. delete
2. autobiography
3. collaborate
4. nape
5. interject
6. redundancy
7. cliché
8. fad
9. consider
10. vacillate
11. stature
12. repetitive
13. prevalent
14. superfluous
15. pitfall

Crossword Puzzle

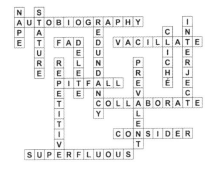

Lesson 10

Ex. B

1. a) maintain
2. b) nondescript
3. d) entreat
4. c) timorously
5. b) sneer

Ex. C

1. O humble, pretentious
2. S degrading, embarrassing
3. S veritable, true
4. S hunker, crouch
5. S ragamuffin, pauper

Ex. D

1. entreat
2. alms
3. ragamuffin
4. pauper
5. timorously
6. nondescript
7. flat
8. hunker
9. humble
10. maintain
11. cringe
12. degrading
13. veritable
14. pretentious
15. sneer

Crossword Puzzle

Lesson 11

Ex. B

1. b) dilemma
2. d) insolent
3. c) fathom
4. a) rogue
5. b) degenerate

Ex. C

1. S timorously, timidly
2. O scornfully, lovingly
3. S retrieve, regain
4. O honesty, guile
5. S confounded, confused

Ex. D

1. fathom
2. scruffy
3. degenerate
4. indignant
5. grapple
6. address
7. ambivalence
8. timidly
9. confounded
10. insolent
11. scornfully
12. guile
13. retrieve
14. dilemma
15. rogue

Crossword Puzzle

Lesson 12

Ex. B

1. d) biology
2. d) seismograph
3. c) cryptograph
4. a) hyperventilate
5. b) pandemic

Ex. C

1. S amorphous, shapeless
2. O respectively, randomly
3. O passion, apathy
4. S perimeter, outline
5. S panacea, cure-all

Ex. D

1. panacea
2. respectively
3. perimeter
4. altimeter
5. biology
6. apathy
7. autograph
8. pandemic
9. graphology
10. amorphous
11. hyperventilate
12. originate
13. seismograph
14. cryptograph
15. geology

Crossword Puzzle

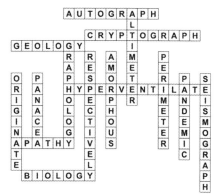

Lesson 13

Ex. B

1. d) gastronomy
2. b) gauche
3. a) indulgence
4. c) mousse
5. a) appetizer

Ex. C

1. S adulation, worship
2. S main course, entrée
3. S restaurateur, owner
4. S potable, drinkable
5. O sautéed, raw

Ex. D

1. culinary
2. indulgence
3. potable
4. sautéed
5. gastronomy
6. restaurateur
7. adulation
8. à la carte
9. chef
10. appetizer
11. soufflé
12. gauche
13. entrée
14. mousse
15. gustatory

Crossword Puzzle

Lesson 14

Ex. B

1. c) sparse
2. c) solitary
3. b) inanimate
4. a) desolate
5. d) denizen

Ex. C

1. S forsaken, abandoned
2. S indigenous, native
3. S deceive, belie
4. O stalwart, fragile
5. O deceptive, true

Ex. D

1. fickle
2. stalwart
3. solitary
4. denizen
5. desolate
6. forsaken
7. sparse
8. habitation
9. inherent
10. indigenous
11. communal
12. belie
13. inanimate
14. agitation
15. deceptive

Crossword Puzzle

Lesson 15

Ex. B

1. d) clamber
2. a) subterranean
3. c) abode
4. b) aura
5. d) frenetic

Ex. C

1. S banquet, repast
2. O stroll, scuttle
3. S scatter, dispel
4. O prickle, soothe
5. S unequivocally, undoubtedly

Ex. D

1. dispel
2. unequivocally
3. intrinsic
4. emanate
5. quietude
6. subterranean
7. repast
8. misstep
9. frenetic
10. prickle
11. clamber
12. predator
13. scuttle
14. aura
15. abode

Crossword Puzzle

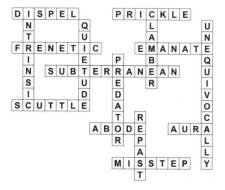

Lesson 16
Ex. B
1. a) choleric
2. b) intense
3. d) motley
4. c) ameliorate
5. c) irony

Ex. C
1. O excess, moderation
2. O coarse, suave
3. S bold, audacious
4. S enchanting, charming
5. O disparate, identical

Ex. D
1. prudent
2. enchanting
3. trait
4. assuage
5. ameliorate
6. pit
7. irony
8. intense
9. choleric
10. suave
11. moderation
12. disparate
13. audacious
14. dynamics
15. motley

Crossword Puzzle
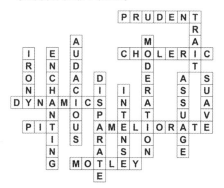

Lesson 17
Ex. B
1. c) docile
2. b) frolic
3. a) anecdote
4. b) disruption
5. d) tether

Ex. C
1. S bold, intrepid
2. O profusion, scarcity
3. S execute, complete
4. S frenzy, pandemonium
5. O guest, interloper

Ex. D
1. devastation
2. frolic
3. profusion
4. tether
5. irresistible
6. conjure
7. whiff
8. docile
9. intrepid
10. anecdote
11. execute
12. disruption
13. escapade
14. pandemonium
15. interloper

Crossword Puzzle
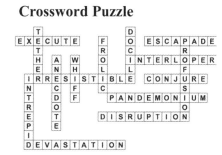

Lesson 18
Ex. B
1. b) ardor
2. c) apparatus
3. a) contraption
4. d) ransack
5. d) feasible

Ex. C
1. O optimism, doubt
2. O miscellany, sets
3. O flout, comply
4. O hypothesis, fact
5. S dauntless, determined

Ex. D
1. dauntless
2. flout
3. feasible
4. buoyant
5. physics
6. miscellany
7. ardor
8. comprise
9. scavenge
10. apparatus
11. scour
12. optimism
13. contraption
14. hypothesis
15. ransack

Crossword Puzzle

Lesson 19
Ex. B
1. d) appendage
2. c) would-be
3. a) cumbersome
4. b) bevy
5. c) utility

Ex. C
1. O homely, garish
2. O precarious, invincible
3. S obscure, unclear
4. S frenzy, bedlam
5. S hodgepodge, miscellany

Ex. D
1. convene
2. bedlam
3. homely
4. bevy
5. mariner
6. device
7. lug
8. cumbersome
9. appendage
10. would-be
11. obscure
12. utility
13. garish
14. hodgepodge
15. precarious

Crossword Puzzle

Ex. D

1. recount
2. enthrall
3. folklore
4. benign
5. stilted
6. uproarious
7. dialect
8. identify
9. cadence
10. eerie
11. innate
12. intonation
13. misadventure
14. mannerism
15. regale

Lesson 20

Ex. B

1. c) enthrall
2. d) benign
3. a) dialect
4. b) identify
5. c) recount

Ex. C

1. S stilted, rigid
2. O eerie, reassuring
3. S misadventure, accident
4. S cadence, rhythm
5. S regale, amuse

Crossword Puzzle

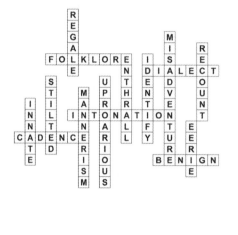